Jas. McGregor Bertram

S^T. HELENA

AND

THE CAPE OF GOOD HOPE.

S^T. HELENA.

NEW YORK

EDWARD H. FLETCHER.

1852.

ST. HELENA

AND

THE CAPE OF GOOD HOPE:

OR,

INCIDENTS IN THE MISSIONARY LIFE

OF THE

REV. JAMES M'GREGOR BERTRAM,

OF ST. HELENA.

BY REV. EDWIN F. HATFIELD, D.D.,
PASTOR OF THE SEVENTH PRESBYTERIAN CHURCH IN THE CITY OF NEW YORK.

With an Introduction,
BY REV. GEORGE B. CHEEVER, D.D.,
PASTOR OF THE CHURCH OF THE PURITANS, NEW YORK.

NEW YORK:
PUBLISHED BY EDWARD H. FLETCHER,
141 NASSAU STREET.
1852.

N. Y. STEREOTYPE ASSOCIATION,
201 William-street.

TO THE

FRIENDS OF MISSIONS,

OF VARIOUS EVANGELICAL CHURCHES IN THE UNITED STATES, WHO HAVE SO NOBLY RESPONDED TO

MR. BERTRAM'S APPEALS,

AND SO GENEROUSLY CONTRIBUTED TO THE ERECTION OF CHURCHES ON

"The Rock of the Ocean,

THIS HUMBLE MEMOIR IS AFFECTIONATELY INSCRIBED BY

THE AUTHOR.

PREFACE.

To those who have heard, from the lips of the Rev. James M'Gregor Bertram, of St. Helena, the particulars of his missionary experience at Table and Saldanha Bays, in the South of Africa, and on the Island of St. Helena, no apology need be offered for the publication of this memoir. It has been written, in compliance with frequent and pressing solicitations on the part of many of his hearers, who regard his statements as worthy of more than the fleeting publicity of a pulpit address, and who desire some lasting memorial of a visit, which they will ever remember with pleasure.

Mr. Bertram came to this country in the year 1850, landing at Boston on the 10th of July, and has visited numerous places in the New England States, New York, New Jersey, Pennsylvania, Maryland, and elsewhere, in the prosecution of his work of benevolence. Six thousand dollars were wanted for the erection of two mission chapels, and the removal of a mortgage upon another, in the Island of St. Helena, in addition to what had been contributed by the friends of the Gospel on the Island, and at the Cape of Good Hope. Wherever he has gone, and addressed the people in this behalf, he has met with a ready response, and found a goodly company of cheerful givers. In a few more days he hopes to have received the substantial aid, to obtain which he sought these shores, and to set sail, full of gratitude to God and his large-hearted friends in America, for his far-off home in the sea-girt isle, where the illustrious Corsican rested from his brilliant career of conquests, and ended his days in inglorious exile.

The sketches here presented have been derived, for the most part, from the public addresses of Mr. Bertram, and from publications and statements that he has kindly put into the possession of

THE EDITOR.

NEW YORK, *May* 10*th*, 1852.

George B. Cheever, D.D.

INTRODUCTION.

The spectacle of Divine Power in action is always sublime. It is a glorious sight when you look upon the waters of Niagara, and listen to the roar of its thunders; or upon the fall of an Alpine avalanche, as of a mountain from the sky. It is glorious to see the sun rise and set, sublime to see the ocean in a storm, or a volcano in action; still more, to gaze upon the planets in the firmament of heaven, and think of that Infinite Power that keeps them silently rolling in the depths of space, in such countless numbers, yet in such order, harmony, and beauty. But more glorious by far is the spectacle of Divine power and grace in the regeneration of congregated souls. To see a nation, a whole nation, in a space of time only one third the span of human life, one third the span given to the development of individual character, taken from the deepest depths of heathenism, raised up from the unutterable abominations of the most despotic idolatry, from the beastliness of habits of pollution, sanctioned and enforced by the rites of superstition, and to see that nation so changed in that short space of time as to possess and put on all the characteristics of Christian purity and refinement; this is a manifestation of Almighty power more wondrous than the creation of a world! It is, indeed, the standing and startling miracle of modern times—a miracle of wisdom, omnipotence, and love. It shows what the gospel of Christ and the grace of God can do.

This glorious miracle of Divine power and grace has been witnessed in the SANDWICH ISLANDS; and, adorning the same age, and fit to be set in the same record, though on a smaller scale, is the miracle of God's power and mercy, of which some account is given in this volume, wrought, or begun to be wrought, in the Island of St. Helena. Truly, the island prophecies in the Word of God are coming out into great light and majesty. They are as morning stars of fulfillment before the Great Sun of Righteousness pours His beams on all the nations.

And these prophecies are fulfilled in so extraordinary a manner, as to reveal with great clearness and power the manner in which the Lord Jesus causes His strength to be perfected and glorified in human weakness, when there is only a simple and strong faith in Him. These records of transactions in the island world, that may have caused greater wonder and joy in heaven than all the transactions in the same space of time elsewhere evolved on our globe, show the sublimity of faith, and the important part it must ever bear, in subduing a fallen world to Christ Jesus. It is faith in God, on man's part, whereby He will accomplish His purposes; or, rather, this faith in God, and the heavenly courage produced by it, giving glory to Him, constitute the disposition, in behalf of which, and in the exercise of which, God can, with justice to Himself and lasting good to His creatures, make bare the arm of His power, and lead His children to victory. They shall have the victory when their heart is fixed on Him, and their eye single to His glory. For God will make His people and the world understand and feel that great principle of holiness and glory, of victory and success, *not by might nor by power, but by the Spirit of the Lord of Hosts.*

When that is understood and acted upon—when God's people rely boldly and only upon Him, then one of them can chase a thousand, and two put ten thousand to flight. Let them go forth, armed with God's Word, fervent in prayer, relying on the Holy Spirit, crying out with the good King Asa, "Lord God, this cause is not ours, but thine, and these enemies are not ours, but thine; let not man prevail against THEE!" and then shall the hosts of darkness be scattered, and the Church of God shall shine forth fair as the moon, clear as the sun, and terrible as an army with banners. But let them not be afraid of God's Word, nor of the application of it, for it is by that alone that error and iniquity can be conquered; for the weapons of our warfare are not carnal, but spiritual, and mighty, through God, to the pulling down of strong-holds. "Hearken unto me, ye that know righteousness, the people in whose heart is my law. Fear ye not the reproach of men, neither be ye afraid of their revilings. For the moth shall eat them up like a garment, and the worm shall eat them like wool; but my righteousness shall be forever, and my salvation from generation to generation." "Who art thou, that thou shouldst be afraid of a man that shall die, and of the son of man, which shall be made as grass, and forgettest the Lord thy maker, that hath stretched forth the heavens and laid the foundations of the earth, and hast feared continually every day, because of the fury of the oppressor, as if he were ready to destroy; and where is the fury of the oppressor? I am the Lord thy God, that divided the sea, whose waves roared. And I have put my words in thy mouth, and have covered thee in the shadow of my hand, that I may plant the heavens and lay the foundations of the earth, and say unto Zion, Thou art my people!" Yes! for this it is that God hath given His Word, and covers His people while they proclaim it, that the world may be con vinced of sin, and conquered by it, and a church built up, who are the people of the living God—the revealers and partakers of His righteousness. Therefore, let His people be faithful *with* His Word; let them trust in it, and in God who gave it, and let them never be afraid of it. There is nothing lost by faithfulness; there is every thing gained by boldness.

We think this is strikingly manifested in this record of the work of God in St. Helena. God prepared His instrument in that work by faith; childlike, simple, unquestioning, unhesitating, God impelled him forth, and God went with him. It really reminds us —this spiritual conquest in that rocky, sea-girt isle— of the expedition—apparently wild and romantic, and the success and the victory, manifestly from God, as the impulse was from His Spirit—of Jonathan, when he went alone to the garrison of the Philistines. "And Jonathan said to the young man that bare his armor, Come, and let us go over unto the garrison of these uncircumcised. It may be that the Lord will work for us. For there is no restraint to the Lord, to save by many or by few."

How admirable! How worthy of all imitation

and praise! This was not the native courage of the warrior only, but the fearlessness of the Christian, relying on his God. *It may be that the Lord will work for us.* How humble, simple, childlike, and beautiful is his faith! He does not pretend to certainty, does not profess to have met God in a dream, or to have had any special revelation from Him, as the ground of his confidence, or any assurance that he should be successful in the present case. But the effort was worth making, and it might be that God would give it success; at any rate, they were not to sit still, and venture nothing. Something was worth hazarding in the cause of God, and if they never attempted any thing without being first sure of success, they never would gain any thing. Jonathan was willing to leave the event with God; and, trusting in God, his conduct was boldness, but not rashness.

Boldness in the cause of God is prudence. If the path of any enterprise be the path of duty, then dismiss your fears, and go forward, leaving the result with God. You need ask for nothing more than this young Christian warrior's humble confidence and willingness. *It may be that the Lord will work for us.* Suppose He should not, what then? Is the doubt or the fear that He will not, a good ground for relinquishing an effort, where you may accomplish great things for God? Does the fear that God will not work for you, release you from the obligation of working for Him? You must be willing to work on a *may-be.* Positive assurance of success is not to be demanded; and if men wait for that, they will do nothing, undertake nothing. Enterprises begun in faith are most successful. It is right to count the cost, but, after all, you must throw yourself on God; and the fear of the cost of a possible failure ought not to hold you back from a possible success. *It may be.* If you do not undertake it, it certainly will *not* be. God will not work for you, if you do not give Him opportunity; but if you do, He may. If you hazard nothing, for fear that He will not work, you are a great coward, and it is a very selfish plan that you go upon. Jonathan committed himself to the Lord's cause, quite regardless of his own interests. It was truly a sublime sight to see him cast himself on God, and go forth on such a desperate undertaking, quite willing to meet all the hazard, quite forgetful of self, and ready to make any sacrifice, for the sake of accomplishing, possibly, a great thing for his country, by God's help. *It may be that God will work for us;* we will go, at any rate. If He *does* work for us, we shall do a *great* work; we will not let the possibility of His *not* working enter into our calculation.

Now, that was not only true courage, but true wisdom, as genuine courage always is. It was a true missionary spirit. It was just in this way that our devoted missionaries to the Sandwich Islands and to India went forth first, against such incalculable odds, with nothing but God to rely upon. *It may be that God will work for us.* The supposition that He will not, shall not enter into our calculation. But even if He does not, the effort is for Him, and cannot be lost. Fruitless it may be, but lost, or disregarded, or forgotten of God, it cannot be. It will be precious in His sight, it will meet His approbation. Even supposing that we die in the midst of it, is it not a death for God? Do we not give ourselves up to Him? The path of duty is the path of safety, though death itself stood in the way; but in a battle, the boldest are the safest, and they are the most likely to come off uninjured.

This was a true *revival* spirit—an example of what may be done, even by one man, with great faith, in a time of insensibility and lukewarmness. *It may be.* There was no beginning of a revival of courage or of piety in the army; there were no extraordinary signs. The beginning of the work was in Jonathan's own heart: all things externally looked discouraging. But Jonathan said, *It may be.* Who knows? There is this great work to be accomplished, and perhaps God will use us to accomplish it. Indeed, we are only two or three, but that is nothing against the enterprise, if God be with us. *It may be that the Lord will work for us, for there is no restraint to the Lord, to save by many or by few.* It was a mode of argument taught by the Spirit of God; it was a divine inspiration in Jonathan's soul—the inspiration of faith, a strong sense of the presence and power of God, an entire reliance upon Him, and a most sincere and fervent desire for God's glory.

These are the graces that indicate and prove an appointed work from God. In moving under these impulses, Jonathan could hardly be presumptuous, or in danger of mistake as to the path of duty. Indeed, the path of duty was clear, and the only question was, would Jonathan do right to venture upon it so entirely alone, and without human assistance? But Jonathan knew that whether with or without human assistance, except by the blessing of God, he could do nothing; and he also knew that the less there was of man, the more sometimes there was of God. Just so David felt when he went against Goliah. It was an undertaking that seemed, in the judgment of some men, merely presumptuous and foolhardy, not to say ridiculous, and the more so, because David refused to be girded with Saul's armor. Sometimes the things that the men of the world rely upon, and by which they expect every thing to be accomplished, and without which they think nothing can be done, are mere impediments to faith.

For the illustration of these lessons, we refer to the interesting and instructive narrative in the following pages. It is a narrative that utters in every part the anthem of brighter worlds—Glory to God and the Lamb! It is a narrative that shows what God may at any time be pleased to do, inspiring the weakness of man; and what man may do, trusting in the strength of God. To the Christian at home and the missionary abroad, it is a narrative full of heavenly suggestion and encouragement.

The relation of it to the churches in America has gained Mr. Bertram and his island mission a place of remembrance and affectionate prayerful interest in thousands of hearts, that otherwise would have heard of this great work of grace only by faint and far-off voices. What has been given, has been given joyfully; never did any appeal for any station in the wide missionary field of the world meet a more welcome response, and prayer has gone before the offering.

CONTENTS.

Edwin F. Hatfield D.D.

LIFE AND LABORS.

CHAPTER I.

LIFE AT HOME.

James M'Gregor Bertram is a native of Scotland. He was born February 24th, 1806, at Southfield, in the parish of Gladsmuir, East Lothian, Haddingtonshire, where, a hundred years ago, the great historian, Dr. William Robertson, ministered in the name of Christ, and where he wrote his "History of Scotland." The home of his childhood was in the western part of the parish, not far from the village of Tranent, and in full view of the majestic Frith of Forth, which is reached by an easy descent of land toward the North. Preston Pans, where Charles Edward Stuart, the Pretender, having already taken Edinburgh, met and completely routed the forces of Sir John Cope, on the morning of Saturday, the 21st of September, 1745, on which occasion the godly Colonel James Gardiner lost his life, is in the immediate neighborhood on the west. The capital is but eleven miles distant. Haddington, where that man of God, the Rev. John Brown, of the Associate Synod, so faithfully taught and illustrated the Gospel, and whose fame is in all the churches, is about four miles to the east. It is a neighborhood full of interest to the lover of Scotch history, and of stirring associations.

The father of Mr. Bertram, true to the faith of his noble ancestors, adhered to the Church of Scotland, and faithfully endeavored to bring up his children (deprived of their godly mother at an early age) in the nurture and admonition of the Lord. He taught them to walk in the fear of God, to reverence His name, to hallow His sabbaths, to study His word, and to offer the morning and evening sacrifice. His children were severally brought to the sanctuary in their infancy, and consecrated to God. JAMES M'GREGOR was thus baptized, according to the usages of the Scottish Church, shortly after his birth, by the Rev. Mr. Brown, in the parish church of Gladsmuir.

In the year 1809 the family removed to the southwest of Scotland, and took up their residence at Mount Pleasant, about half a mile from the ancient town of Dumfries, on the eastern bank of the river Nith, and about nine miles from the Solway Frith. Here in the midst of beautiful scenery and splendid prospects, for which Dumfries is so justly celebrated—here, among the hills and vales of bonny Nithsdale, immortalized by Scotland's favorite bard, where Burns spent the last eight years of his life, and where he was buried, as indicated by the noble monument in St. Michael's church-yard, over his remains—Mr. Bertram passed his youthful days, and grew to the stature of manhood. His worthy sire, shortly after his arrival at Dumfries, became connected with the Relief Church, then under the pastoral care of the venerable Andrew Fife, by whose ministrations the religious impressions, made on the youthful mind of James by parental faithfulness, were greatly confirmed. He received the rudiments of learning at an excellent school in Dumfries, but the limited means of the family could not afford him the advantages of a finished education.

The father was a tiller of the ground, on a small scale. He occupied himself principally in the cultivation of plants, and flowers, and seeds; in which healthful and inspiring employment he was assisted by James. His boyhood thus was passed amid the beauties of nature, in close familiarity with some of her most delightful works. He spent his early days, not in the feculent atmosphere of the crowded haunts of vice and dissipation, but in the midst of umbrageous woods, and graceful plants, and smiling flowers,

"Where the fantastic tulip strives to break
In two-fold beauty, and a parted streak;

The twining jasmine and the blushing rose,
With lavish grace their morning scents disclose:
The smelling tuberose and jonquil declare
The stronger impulse of an evening air."

It is a privilege not sufficiently appreciated, to have our earliest associations formed away from the artificial habits, and dusty streets, and dingy walls of the city—away from the thousand temptations that there beset the minds of the youth, and lead them astray—to dwell where God is seen in all His works, and where sweet innocence, simplicity, and purity are found.

"Oh! friendly to the best pursuits of man—
Friendly to thought, to virtue, and to peace,
Domestic life, in rural pleasure passed!
Few know thy value, and few taste thy sweets;
Though many boast thy favors, and affect
To understand and choose thee for their own."

An elder brother had found his way to England, and established himself, in company with Mr. Alexander Grierson, as a cloth merchant, in the flourishing town of Manchester. Thither James was sent in 1824, at the age of eighteen years, to assist his brother Thomas, and learn the art and mystery of trade. Thomas Bertram was a member of the Independent Church, worshiping in Chapel-street, near Gravel-lane, Salford, under the pastoral care of the Rev. John A. Coombs. Occasionally the young Scotchman was found at St.

Clement's Church, Levers-street, at that time served by the Rev. William Nunn. Under the ministry of the latter, in the year 1825, his conscience appears to have been aroused, and his soul awakened to a vivid religious sensibility. The precious seed, that had so long before been sown in Nithsdale, now began to vegetate and bear fruit in Lancashire. He was led to seek the forgiveness of sin and peace with God, through faith in the blood of Jesus Christ. From this time the course of his life was changed. In his nineteenth year he became a subject of grace, and cherished a hope of salvation.

Although Mr. Bertram had thus been brought to regard himself as a believer, he was still by no means decided as to the particular church, in which he should make a profession of religion. It is not necessary to state the considerations which kept him for a length of time from the Lord's table. It was not until the twenty-seventh year of his age that his course was made plain, and the way prepared for his complete separation from the world. In the year 1833, the Rev. ROBERT AITKEN, at that time a preacher of wonderful power and popularity, came to Manchester, and exerted, by the blessing of God, that influence over the mind of Mr. Bertram, which resulted in his full and entire consecration to the service of God.

This distinguished preacher deserves more than

a passing notice. He is a native of North Britain, having been born at the close of the last century, in Roxburghshire, not far from the Tweed, in Tiviotdale. Sent, by a friend of his father's family, into England, to be educated for the Church, he was introduced into the ranks of the clergy of the Establishment about thirty years ago. Some little time after his admission to orders, he became the incumbent of the chapel at Douglas, a sea-port town on the eastern shore of the Isle of Man, and the principal place on the island, lying about sixty miles in a northwesterly direction from Liverpool. Shortly after, he was united in marriage to a lady of the place, of considerable property and high respectability. For a period of about ten or twelve years, Mr. Aitken continued in the performance of his official duties as a parish priest, respected and flattered by the people, but destitute of the power of godliness. Greatly attached to the Church of England, he held no communion with dissent, and scorned to be found in attendance on the ministrations of a Non-conformist.

It pleased God, however, to make use of an instrumentality so despicable in the sight of the self-righteous clergyman, to bring him to the knowledge of the truth. He made choice, as He so often does, of "the foolish things of the world to confound the wise," and "the weak things of the world to confound the things which are mighty, and base things of the world, and things which are despised." Some time about the year 1831, Mr. Aitken was passing a Wesleyan chapel in the Isle of Man, while the society were occupied in an evening conference. His attention was arrested, and he stopped without, to listen to the artless statements made by the brethren, in the narration of their Christian experience. He heard enough to convince him, that he was an entire stranger to such spiritual exercises, and utterly destitute of that "joy and peace in believing," which seemed to characterize these poor, despised dissenters. As he returned home, the conviction fastened itself upon him that he was a lost sinner. He shut himself up in his study, and began to cry for mercy. His prayer was heard, his pride humbled, his former righteousness renounced, and his heart renewed by Divine grace.

The change thus effected in his views, feelings, desires, hopes, purposes, and plans, was most thorough. Filled to overflowing with the joy of a new convert, his whole countenance glowed with heavenly radiance. He longed to impart the same spiritual gift—instrumentally, at least—to his loved companion. He almost flew to find her, and communicate to her the glad tidings; but he seemed to her as one bereft of reason. At length, however, she too was led to seek the Lord, and became as happy and zealous as himself.

He now entered upon the work of preaching Christ with all his heart and soul. The people soon perceived the change in their minister, and flocked from all quarters to hear from his lips the wonders of Divine grace. The sanctuary was filled to overflowing with the crowds, and great numbers of them were pricked in their hearts, and led to cry, "What shall I do to be saved?" The awakening became general, not only in the town, but in other portions of the island. Taking advantage of the growing excitement, Mr. Aitken went everywhere preaching the word. As the churches were utterly insufficient to receive the multitudes, he adopted the practice of Whitefield and Wesley, and preached under the open canopy of heaven, in the fields, in the streets, and wherever the people could be gathered together. On one of these occasions, the congregation and their preacher were surprised by a heavy shower of rain, and found shelter within a Wesleyan chapel in the neighborhood, where, by the urgent invitation of the proprietors, Mr. Aitken continued and concluded the service. So uncanonical an act could not be overlooked by the Lord Bishop of Sodor and Man. The Right Rev. William Ward, D.D., at once decided, that the man, who could pay so little regard to the canons of the Church, should feel the weight of her ordinances. Mr. Aitken was accordingly removed from his incumbency, and his name erased from the number of the clergy. Such are the tender mercies of lordly prelacy! "From such apostles," God "preserve the Church!"

But the fire thus kindled was not so easily to be quenched. The fame thereof reached Liverpool; and soon an invitation was received from some of the dissenting people of that great commercial mart, and Mr. Aitken made them a visit. He was received with open arms, and invited to the pulpit of the Wesleyan chapel in Pitt-street. The results of his preaching soon appeared, as in the Isle of Man. He possessed a most attractive and commanding person, being fully six feet in height, and well-proportioned; of black hair, and heavy whiskers, with a voice full, powerful, melodious, and perfectly at command. A well-trained mind, of far more than ordinary powers, brought into full exercise by the impulse of the new-born zeal with which his whole soul was fired, aided by vehement but graceful gesticulation, gave him a most wonderful control over the crowds and masses that flocked to hear him. He had seen so much of the deceitfulness of his own heart, that he trembled with apprehension for the vast multitude of professing Christians and others, whom he could not but regard as "having no hope, and without God in the world." He therefore deemed it to be his duty to bring the terrors of the Lord to bear with burning weight upon the ungodly, and so to prevail upon them, if possible, to turn from the error of their ways. He took for his motto, "The sword of the Lord, and of Gideon!" and armed himself for a crusade against all ungodliness. To the wounded sinner he held up a Redeemer crucified, and bade him "Look and live."

Numerous chapels were opened to welcome him, but none were large enough to contain the crowds. Deep impressions were made by the truths that he preached, and many souls were added to the Lord. He went up to London, and preached with like results in White's Row Chapel, Spitalfields, and in other chapels in the metropolis. He visited several of the large provincial towns, and ranged through Yorkshire, where his coming was like a tornado, sweeping all before it. He laid siege particularly to Sheffield, and so mightily prevailed the word of the Lord, that no less than six thousand souls, as was thought, were awakened to seek the Lord. At Birmingham and Manchester also, the populace were stirred, and ran to hear this second Whitefield. A wonderful revival of religion attended his ministrations wherever he went, and his fame spread abroad through all the land. His services were in great request, and his labors almost superhuman.

Measures were taken by some of the Scotch

residents of Liverpool, in 1835, to induce Mr. Aitken to locate himself among them. In conference with him, they pledged themselves to co-operate with him in a vigorous assault on the ungodliness and hypocrisy of the town, and to furnish the means for his support, and for the erection of a suitable place of worship. A commodious hall in Cook-street, capable of seating about eight hundred persons, was rented, and immediately opened for public worship. Ground was also obtained in Hope-street, and the foundations of a house of worship speedily laid.

About this time Mr. Bertram's acquaintance with Mr. Aitken commenced. The latter had visited Manchester on a preaching excursion, and, as usual, attracted vast multitudes. A worthy Scotch citizen, at whose house Mr. Aitken was entertained, invited Mr. Bertram to his house, and introduced him as an ardent-minded Christian, whose views and sympathies were in unison with those of the distinguished preacher. The mind of Mr. Bertram had long been turning toward the work of the ministry, and he was anxiously desirous to learn the path of duty. In Mr. Aitken he found an ardent friend and faithful counselor. A mutual attachment was formed, which led to a frequent correspondence on the return of Mr. Aitken to Liverpool. At the end of six months, Mr. Bertram concluded to listen to the pressing invitation of his friend, to go down to Liverpool, and take up his abode in the hospitable mansion of Mr. Aitken, with a view to prepare himself for the gospel ministry. After his removal, he gave himself to the work of exhorting, instructing, and praying in the social meetings of the new society.

Hope-street Chapel was completed in 1836, and dedicated to the worship of God about five months after the foundations were laid. It was of respectable appearance, built of stone, and adapted for the accommodation of about two thousand persons. It was immediately filled, and continued to be filled to overflowing. Month after month the Spirit of God was poured upon the congregation, and great numbers were hopefully converted to God. In ten months, the society, which had been organized with only nine members, had increased to fifteen hundred, of whom twelve hundred had been gathered out of the world, and received into the church on the relation of their experience. The work had extended into other towns. In Manchester, Burslem, Hanley, Congleton, Preston, and Leigh, where Mr. Aitken had occasionally preached, little bands of brethren had gathered around him. It was desirable that these stations should be occupied. Accordingly, Mr. Bertram, with three other zealous brethren, Messrs. Campbell, Delaney, and Read, were publicly set apart, in the summer of 1836, to the work of the ministry.

At a convocation held in Hope-street Chapel, October 27th, 1836, in which the several stations were fully represented, it was resolved to form themselves into a society, to be called "The Christian Society in connection with the Rev. R. Aitken." Rules and regulations were adopted, and the policy as well as purpose of the new organization defined. It was agreed that, while the word of God alone should be regarded as the only infallible standard of their faith, "Wesley's Sermons and Notes on the New Testament" should be considered as containing their "sentiments of doctrinal truth," and be adopted as their legal and scriptural standard of doctrine; although the views of the body were rather more Calvinistic than this would indicate. An ecclesiastical polity, compounded mainly of the Wesleyan and Presbyterian systems, was also adopted, and experimental piety made an indispensable prerequisite to membership. They determined to be "a working, soul-saving society;" to make the salvation of souls the one great object and business of the association; to labor and pray for revivals of religion, and to seek for mighty effusions of the Holy Spirit. Prayer meetings were to be held weekly, and oftener, ıı possible, and to be so multiplied as to give abundant opportunities for every one of the members to exercise their gifts of prayer. After every evening service, penitent meetings, or, as we call them, inquiry meetings, were to be held. The sermons were to be "not neatly-composed essays to amuse the intellect, but plain, strong, pointed appeals to awaken the conscience. The lazy, useless system of talking about good things in the pulpit," was to "be totally discarded, and every minister" required to "throw his body, soul, and spirit into the work." At the penitent meetings, "the elders and leaders" were to "go from pew to pew and exhort sinners to repentance." Gayety of dress, parties of pleasure, the use of intoxicating drinks, except as medicine, and marriage with unconverted persons, were not to be allowed, and all were conscientiously to observe private, family, and public worship. In the admission of members, no true Christian was to be rejected on account of any peculiarity of doctrinal views.

Such was the frame-work of a society which, within a few years, exerted a large influence in the work of calling sinners to repentance. The doctrinal views of Mr. Aitken and the preachers in the connection, almost coincided with those of the Rev. Charles G. Finney, of Ohio, an edition of whose "Revival Lectures" he put to the press, with an Introduction, "vindicating and enforcing

Mr. Finney's plan of conducting the work of God."

Immediately after the convocation, Mr. Bertram removed to the market-town of Hanley, near the sources of the Trent, near Newcastle-under-Lyne, in the northern part of Staffordshire, to which station he had been appointed, in connection with Mr. Delaney. Here, among the potteries, with which the region is studded, he found ample employment for his ministerial gifts. Two churches were organized, and a number of out-stations were established. At the expiration of a year he was removed to Doncaster, an ancient and beautiful town in the southern part of Yorkshire, on the southeastern bank of the river Don, about eighteen miles northeast of Sheffield, and famous for its races. Here, too, his ministry was prospered, and a church of about one hundred members was gathered. In the fall of 1838 he was appointed to Stockport, a large and flourishing town, exceedingly picturesque, on both sides of the Mersey, and lying partly in Cheshire and partly in Lancashire, only seven miles from his former residence in Manchester, to the southeast. Here, too, he found a wide field of usefulness among the numerous workmen employed in the cotton factories, for which the town is famous. His ministry was much prospered, and a church of three hundred souls was gathered in the course of twelve months. From Stockport he removed in the autumn of 1839 to the city of Bristol, where he labored for the two years following in connection with the Rev. John Richardson, and gathered two churches, one containing about two hundred, and the other about three hundred members.

During his residence in Bristol, his views on the mode of baptism were considerably modified. To this subject his attention was called by the preaching of the Rev. Thomas Matthews, of Bedford. After a short season of inquiry, he concluded to offer himself as a candidate for immersion ; and with his wife, the Rev. Mr. Richardson, and several others, he was accordingly immersed in the year 1838, by the Rev. John Bowes, of Dundee, without forfeiting, by this proceeding, his standing in the connection. He adopted mainly the views of the great Robert Hall, and a large portion of our Baptist brethren in England, on the subject of church fellowship.

In the mean time, Mr. Aitken, and the other ministers in the connection, were laboring, full of zeal and energy, in the prosecution of what they deemed to be their particular mission.

Mr. Aitken had procured, in 1838, the old chapel in White's Row, Spitalfields, in the eastern part of London, where formerly the venerable Dr. Townsend ministered. Leaving Hope-street Chapel, in Liverpool, to be supplied by others, he removed to the metropolis, and, assisted by Mr. Delaney, conducted the services in White's Row Chapel, producing here, as elsewhere, a great sensation. In the latter part of the same year, he purchased a commodious and comfortable place of worship on the Surry side, called Zion Chapel, Waterloo Road. In both of these chapels, service was maintained twice every Sabbath day, and frequently on the evenings of other days in the week. Immense crowds of all classes were attracted to hear Mr. Aitken, and a great excitement was produced.

Shortly after his removal to London, he was deprived of his wife by death. This excellent lady had proved her devotion to the cause of her Lord and Master by unwearied services. She was regarded by the preachers and the people as a mother in Israel. Her influence over her husband was highly salutary and sanctifying. As long as she lived the work prospered; but, after her death, it was soon perceived that Mr. Aitken was disposed to make his court to the great, the fashionable, and the wealthy. A part of the service of the Church of England, hitherto entirely discarded, was introduced into Zion Chapel. The solemn tones of the organ, too, swept by the fingers of his sister, accompanied the songs of praise. Great offense was given to the society by these innovations. It was soon rumored that he was about to make his peace with the Church, and abandon his late associates. An unmarried lady, of title and large fortune, the Hon. Miss G., was seen to be invariable in attendance on his ministry. It was not long before this lady obtained a complete ascendency over him, and urged upon him the desirableness of his entering the Church, in order to rouse the Establishment, and promote as great a revival within, as he had for years without. It is possible, and so it was said, that the hope of a miter was held out to him. The temptation prevailed. He resolved to conform. His obeisance was made and accepted. He was enjoined to make his confession, and be publicly rebuked. This humiliating scene took place in his own chapel in Liverpool, which he succeeded in carrying over with him. The rebuke was administered by the Rev. Hugh M'Neile, the gifted and popular rector of St. Jude's, Liverpool. It was an occasion of great mortification to the godly men and women who had so long been associated with him in promoting the work of God. Thousands reproached him for his Sampson-like course, in betraying the cause of his Master for another Delilah.

The Honorable Miss G. became the wife of the Rev. Robert Aitken, and introduced her husband to the gentry and nobles, among whom she herself had hitherto moved. He resumed his ministry in

Hope-street Chapel, but "he wist not that the Lord was departed from him." The people no longer thronged the house as in other days. The unction, the power, the soul, were gone. The chapel was almost deserted. Despised by the people whom he had betrayed for a woman, he soon grew wearied of Liverpool, and sought another place of service. A church in Leeds, the great woolen metropolis, was in want of a minister, and Mr. Aitken obtained the situation. It is understood that, in conformity, he now out-Herods Herod, and is verging even upon Popery itself. He is an Anglo-Catholic of the Oxford school, and quite enamored with "The Tracts for the Times." During the ten years immediately succeeding his conversion, he was valiant for the truth, and reaped a rich harvest of souls. Thousands on thousands were awakened under his fervid appeals to seek the Lord, and great numbers were hopefully converted. But for the last ten years his name has seldom been heard, and never in connection with spiritual awakenings and revivals of religion. Sad and impressive is the lesson derived from his experience. It was love for "this present world," that drew a Demas away from Paul and his Master. Like the royal lion, the Rev. Mr. Aitken made his voice to be heard, full of power, majesty, and grandeur; but "a dart strikes through his liver," and he drops, is seized and tamed, no more to strike terror into the hearts of the wicked—no more to sound an alarm in Zion. Mournful spectacle! Alas! that such instances are not more rare.

The defection of their leader disheartened the greater part of the brethren associated with him, and they separated. Many of them became connected with other dissenting bodies, and continued to serve God in the ministry, carrying, in many cases, their churches with them. A small number of them, however, resolved not to abandon the "soul-saving" work to which they had devoted their lives. They accordingly combined, and formed an Association, entitled, "The Ebenezer Christian Missionary Society." The object of the new organization was set forth as having special relation to the preaching of the Gospel in the large manufacturing and sea-port towns, principally in the North of England. Mr. Bertram adhered to this missionary band, and united with them in this organization.

Mr. Bertram now removed to the large and flourishing town of Newcastle, on the northern bank of the river Tyne, in Northumberland, so long renowned for its collieries. Here, and at North Shields, and South Shields—both of them at the mouth of the Tyne, about eight miles to the east of Newcastle—he labored effectively in the ministry some two or three years. He spent about nine months, in 1842–3, on Holy Island, about six miles southeast of Berwick-upon-Tweed, lying near the coast of Northumberland, in the German Ocean, about nine miles in circumference. It is inhabited mostly by fishermen, whom he found in a very neglected state, and among whom he obtained about fifty seals to his ministry. He returned thence to Newcastle, and, after a short residence, revisited the home of his fathers in Dumfries.

A period of almost nine years had now elapsed since his consecration to the work of the ministry. The whole period had been fully occupied in arduous and self-denying labors, principally among the poor and the destitute. He had been a missionary from the beginning; nor had he labored in vain. Hundreds of precious souls, among the thousands to whom he had ministered, had been, through his instrumentality, brought from darkness to light; while to many more he had administered consolation and instruction in the Lord, to their edification and growth in grace. Nor had he wearied of his work; he delighted in it—he gloried in it. It was a source of increasing delight to him, and a perpetual occasion for gratitude to God.

But he had come to regard himself as under a call to a field of labor still more self-denying and laborious. The thrilling appeals from foreign missionaries, for more laborers, had reached his heart. As he listened occasionally to the artless and forcible statements made by some of these brethren, who had returned to their native land to recruit their exhausted health, worn down by unceasing exertions among the wretched, the ignorant, and the debased heathen, his spirit was stirred within him, and his heart panted to carry the glad tidings of the Gospel to the most benighted of Adam's race. At home he saw that thousands of godly ministers were ready to break the bread of life to the hungry, while millions of the heathen world had none to care for their souls.

He could not rid himself of the conviction, that duty called him to labor among the heathen. In the strength of the God of Jacob, he at length resolved to leave his native land, and the friends of his youth, and the homes of civilization, for some pagan shore. He withdrew, in consequence, from the society, under whose auspices he had latterly labored. The field of its operations was at home; they sent no missionaries abroad. In closing their connection with him, they gave him the following testimonial:

"*Ebenezer Christian Missionary Society.*

[Official.]

"This is to certify, that I have been intimately acquainted, and labored in the ministry with the

Rev. James M'Gregor Bertram for the last seven years, during which time he has maintained a character becoming the Gospel of our Lord Jesus Christ. As it respects his ministerial qualifications, they are of a superior order; and whenever he preached, there was invariably an overflowing congregation. His zeal in the cause of God is almost unbounded; and his success in winning souls to Christ has been such that I believe hundreds shall be the crown of his rejoicing when the redeemed are gathered home. And I humbly pray that God may direct him to that sphere of labor where he will be most useful, and where he will be recompensed for his valuable labors.

"J. D. Richardson,
"Corresponding Secretary,
"And Pastor of the Church, South Shields.

"South Shields, *October 26th*, 1844."

CHAPTER II.

LIFE AT "THE CAPE."

THE visit of Mr. Bertram to Dumfries, in 1844, determined the course of his future life. He had formed a matrimonial connection, the result of a youthful attachment, with Mary, the daughter of Mr. Jonathan Currie, a respectable citizen of Dumfries. Three children were born to them in Hanley, Stockport, and Manchester—a daughter and two sons. Mrs. Bertram, whose health required close attention, had left her husband at Newcastle-upon-Tyne, in the spring of 1844, and, with her children, had spent the summer season among the scenes and friends of her childhood in Nithsdale. Mr. Bertram rejoined them in the following autumn.

As the days were passing pleasantly along, in the midst of their kindred, and in the renewal of former friendships, Mr. Bertram very casually, as it would seem to all but reflecting minds, called one day at the counting-house, or ware-room, of Mr. James Afleck, with whom he entered into a free conversation on the subject which had lately so interested his own mind—the work of missions among the heathen.

Perceiving that the mind of Mr. Bertram was very fully set on going abroad, Mr. Afleck says to him, "Come, now, if you wish to go out to the heathen, here is a fine chance for you; the brig Luna, Capt. Carmichael, is lying down at the wharf, taking in a cargo for the Cape of Good Hope. She sails in about a fortnight, and a Major M'Kee goes out in her with his family, so that you will have good company by the way. She is owned by the house of Afleck, Turner, and Co., and, I dare say, your brother-in-law, Thomas Currie, will see my brother Samuel, one of the owners, and secure a passage for yourself and family."

To this proposal he had no reply. It seemed to him, as he thought of it, that the hand of God was in it. He went away, and pondered it in his heart. The more he thought of it, the more was it impressed upon his mind, that God was calling him to embark in this vessel for the scene of his future missionary labors. The business, however, required haste. He could not keep it long in abeyance. The brig was soon to set sail, and the decision must be made without delay.

But this was not the only avenue of usefulness that was opened to him. A chapel, that had been occupied by an Independent Church, in Dumfries, was now vacant. The friends of himself and wife were anxious to retain him among them. They proposed to him the gathering of a congregation on the banks of the Nith, and offered to secure the vacant chapel for the enterprise. The proposition was attractive. It spread before him a beautiful vista of pleasant scenes and delightful prospects. It would have been exceedingly grateful to all the family and friends, as well as gratifying to himself. But he could not rid himself of the conviction, that this was not to be his abiding-place. He carried the matter, day by day, to the throne of grace, and seemed to hear a voice from the inner sanctuary, saying to him and his, "Arise ye, and depart; for this is not your rest." His doubts were solved; his purpose formed. He resolved to put himself under the guidance of the "fiery, cloudy pillar," and obey the voice divine.

Immediately, therefore, he set himself to the work of arranging for his departure in the Luna. He made known his intention to his companion, who, if she did not regard him as already a victim of "*Luna*"-*cy*, thought him in great danger of it. But repeated representations of the case secured at length her assent and coöperation. He then sought another interview with Mr. Afleck, and told him of the result of the conversation which they had had together a few days before. Mr. Afleck consented to break the matter to Mr. Currie, Mr. Bertram's wife's brother, whose circumstances were such as enabled him to help the would-be voyagers on their way, if he should approve of their course. But Mr. Currie was one of your prudent, worldly-wise men, that are wont to have great faith in the old proverb, "A bird in the hand is worth two in the bush." He had never approved of the roving life that his sister had led, and very plainly told her and her husband, that it was high time for them to settle down, and lead a more quiet life. Mrs. Currie, the widowed mother of Mrs. Bertram, an excellent lady, attached to the Church of Scotland, and a worthy member of the kirk, united with her son Thomas in these representations. But when they saw that the heart of Mr. Bertram was fully set in him to go to the heathen, they "ceased; saying, The will of the Lord be done!"

Through the good offices of Mr. Currie, a passage was secured for Mr. Bertram, his wife, and two youngest children, in the brig, for the Cape of Good Hope, the expense of which Mr. Currie paid from his own purse. He also furnished them with a very suitable outfit, valued at about one hundred pounds. Their eldest child, a son, was left with Mr. Bertram's sister, Mrs. James Hamilton, at Manchester, who had ever shown a great fondness for him, and desired to retain and bring him up as her own, having had the charge of him since he was eighteen months old.

The Luna sailed about the first of November, 1844, with Major M'Kee, Mr. Bertram, and their families, as passengers. It might truly be said of the missionary, as it was of the Father of the faithful, that "he went out, not knowing whither he went." No missionary society had taken him under its fostering care, and given him instructions as to his future course. He went at his own charges, so far as his missionary service was concerned. He went forth without purse or scrip, assured that He who feeds the ravens and the sparrows, and clothes the lilies of the field, would give both food and raiment to him and his. Though destitute of all earthly dependence, and having not where to lay his head when he should reach the Cape, he could say, in the sweet words of one of New England's sons:

"Yes, I hasten from you gladly,
From the scenes I love so well;
Far away, ye billows, bear me,
Lovely native land, farewell!
Pleased I leave thee,
Far in heathen lands to dwell."

His fellow-voyagers were, by no means, such as a pious heart would have chosen for companions. The captain and crew, as is so commonly the case, had not the fear of God before their eyes. The most of them were shockingly addicted to profanity, and frequently their oaths and blasphemies could be heard above the howlings of the tempest, with which, on several occasions, the vessel was furiously assailed. Major M'Kee had spent the greater part of his life in the East Indies, in the service of the Hon. East India Company. Having reared a numerous family, he had returned to Scotland, his native land, to spend his declining years in retirement and comfort. But the keen blasts of the North were too severe for a constitution that had so long been tempered by the enervating heat of a torrid clime, and he was compelled to seek a home in a land more congenial to health and life. The Cape of Good Hope, where he had formerly tested the proverbial mildness of the atmosphere, offered him a pleasant home, and thither he had now turned his face. Like the most of those who are bred to arms, the major was as profane as the captain and crew.

The voyagers encountered, as before intimated, a number of terrific storms, of which the last was far the most furious. While the ungodly crew were pouring forth their imprecations, and invoking damnation in their cursings and blasphemies, the missionary betook himself to prayer, fervent and importunate, apprehensive that so much impiety would draw down upon them the vengeance of heaven. His prayers were heard, and, full of gratitude to God for His sparing mercy, he resolved to make a renewed effort for the reform and salvation of those with whom he sailed. He took the captain aside, when the storm had subsided, and remonstrated with him, kindly but faithfully, on the impropriety and wickedness of his course of life. He pursued the same treatment with the first mate. They listened, and were not enraged. Permission was given the missionary to hold, when the weather would permit, during the remainder of the voyage, a daily morning and evening service of prayer, and to preach on the Sabbath.

From this time forward, every morning and evening, the word of God was read in the cabin, and the voice of prayer was heard. The captain, who was by no means a hardened wretch, and whose conscience was quite alive, piped all hands that could be spared from duty, and, with considerable reverence, he and they waited upon the services of their chaplain. On the Sabbath they were no less attentive to the preaching of the word. A marked and delightful change in the deportment of both the officers and their crew soon was manifested. Nor was the change less observable in the cabin. The old East India soldier, who had never, in all his life, save perhaps in childhood, bowed his knee in prayer, became an earnest seeker of the way of salvation. Ere long he might be seen gathering his wife and children around him, reading to them a lesson from the Holy Scriptures; and then, on bended knees, pouring forth his fervent supplications to God in their behalf. The voice of profanity was hushed, and the voice of prayer and praise arose. God was with His servant, and owned his humble labors, while on the way to his destined haven. The concluding part of the voyage was as pleasant as the former part had been trying. Not a few of that company who embarked on the Luna at Dumfries, full of cursing and bitterness, will remember, with eternal gratitude to the Almighty, their happy experience in the South Atlantic Ocean, while they were drawing nigh to the Cape of Good Hope, and beginning, some of them, to entertain a "*good hope*, through grace," of entering a haven of everlasting rest.

At the expiration of the tenth or eleventh week, the wearied voyagers were greeted with the ever-welcome cry of "Land!" The elevated mountain-range, that commences at Table Bay, and stretches some two hundred miles in a northerly direction along the western coast of the southern extremity of Africa, was seen spreading out before their gladdened eyes. As they neared the shore, they could easily distinguish, by its peculiar formation, the huge mass of rock, rising more than three thousand five hundred feet almost directly out of the ocean, whose flattened top has given it the name of "Table Mountain." The "Devil's Peak," an almost conical elevation, towered a little to the left, to the height of more than three thousand three hundred feet; while on the right, and more distant, two peculiar prominences, resembling a crouching lion, to which have been in consequence affixed the name of the "Lion's Head," and the "Lion's Rump," the former nearly two thousand eight hundred feet in height, and the latter more than eleven hundred, completed the background of the noble picture, to which all eyes on board of the Luna were now eagerly directed. They were presently abreast of a beautiful cluster of white villas, bearing the name of Green Point, on their right as they entered the bay, embowered among verdure.

The bay, which also derives its name from the mountain, is approached from the northwest, and is open to the winds that blow from that direction. As these winds prevail most in the winter months, May, June, July, and August, the roadstead—for it can scarcely be called a harbor, for want of a breakwater—is then very insecure, and frequently becomes the scene of great distress. In the month of August, 1842, only two years and a half before Mr. Bertram's arrival, the convict ship "Waterloo," and the transport ship "Abercrombie Robinson," had gone to pieces on the rocks in the bay, when more than a hundred of the convicts found a watery grave. At the southern extremity of the bay, the long line of white houses marks the site of "Cape Town," the principal settlement of the colony of the Cape of Good Hope. It lies on a gently ascending strip of ground, nearly three miles wide, that occupies the space between the mountain and the beach, and is a thriving, busy, and spacious town of more than thirty thousand inhabitants, with its Government-house, Garrison, Forts, Parade-ground, Exchange, churches, chapels, College, schoolhouses, and other public buildings. The Luna had now reached her destination, and her anchor was dropped in the roadstead, among the shipping, some distance from the beach.

As Mr. Bertram and his family were leaving the brig, and were in the act of going over the gangway to enter the boat that was to carry them to the beach, the seamen came crowding around him to bid him farewell. It was hard for them to part with one, whose voice had roused them from the dreadful stupidity that was hurrying them to endless destruction, and awakened within them, by the blessing of God, an earnest desire for the salvation of their souls, through the grace of our Lord Jesus Christ. These hardy sons of the ocean were completely overcome; they wept and sobbed like children. He who had been their ringleader in all mischief and iniquity, the most daring, hardened, and blasphemous wretch among them, John M'Donald, who had grown gray in profanity and dissipation, was now the most affected to tenderness. They could not consent that the missionary should leave them thus, to return to them no more; and so they entreated him to come back to the ship: "We cannot hear of your leaving us, Mr. Bertram," they cried, "unless you promise to come back and preach to us next Sabbath, as you have been in the habit of doing. We never read our Bibles, or thought of our poor souls, or of the Almighty himself, until you came on board the Luna. You must come and preach to us again." Mr. Bertram very readily gave his consent, and assured them that, if it pleased God, he would surely be with them the next Sabbath morning.

It was literally a new world into which our voyagers had been introduced. It seemed strange to them, that the atmosphere was so hot and almost stifling in the month of January; and that the land before them was clothed with the rich verdure and vegetation of midsummer. The habitations also, so low, and so quaint, with their gables to the streets, covered with whitewash, and adorned with green venetians, each with its stoop or porch before it, after the manner of the old Knickerbockers, seemed exceedingly odd. The small window-panes, and the singular sign-boards, and the absence of shop windows, had a singular effect. They were greatly amused at the almost constant serenading of the barn-fowl, and the vast number and variety of lazy dogs, of which no two scarcely were alike. But most of all were they impressed with the strangeness of the people whom they met. At home they had seldom seen a genuine tawny son of Africa; but here they were seen on every hand, and of all descriptions and shades of ebony. They seemed to be the most numerous portion of the population. There were the Hottentots, or "Totties," as they are familiarly called, the aborigines of the territory, of stunted growth, and sallow skin, like "the seared and yellow leaf," not a little bedaubed with grease and filth—with their angular faces, flat noses, high cheek-bones, pouting lips, woolly heads, and small, sunken, twinkling eyes; arrayed in their ragged, thread-bare jackets, leather trowsers, or "crackers," and crumpled, slouching, broad-brimmed straw hats; and their vrouws, as the Dutch call them, of corresponding repulsiveness of person, in their patched and not over-cleanly chintz gowns, and turbans made of crimson cotton handkerchiefs. There, too, was the genuine African negro, of the deepest dye, of woolly hair, and protruding lips, the "galley" of the Cape, the patient bearer of burdens, whose home, or that of his fathers, was Mozambique or Madagascar—once the slave, the property, of the colonist, but now free, and working for him as any other laborers. To these must be added, the swarthy Malays, imported from the East Indies, and commonly known in the British colonies as coolies; a patient, industrious, and useful race, that serve as mechanics, and house-servants, and fishermen. These, and their various intermixtures, swarming everywhere, and mingled with various other African tribes, and the copper-skinned sons of China, and various nondescript specimens of humanity from the far East, of all aspects, of every variety of complexion, and habits of dress, formed a population most singular as well as novel to the newly-arrived. These were the laboring classes, and the lower strata of society.

But hardly less remarkable was the variety among the whites. Of these, a very large proportion they found to be of Dutch descent; the colony having been principally settled by the Lowlanders of Holland, just two hundred years ago (1652), under Dr. John Anthony Van Riebeck, their first governor, and having continued in their possession until the close of the last century. For the last half-century it has been under the British government. The Dutch continue to form the staple of the peasantry, and retain, to a great extent, the primitive manners and customs, as well as the language, of their ancestors of the seventeenth century.

It was curious to observe the singular head-dress, also, to which so many were addicted; the red handkerchiefs with which their heads were bound, in many cases, and the conical straw hats, somewhat resembling inverted funnels; and to see eight or ten yoke of oxen harnessed to a rudely-built wagon, sometimes heavily loaded, but as often with almost nothing in it, like a huge elephant tugging at a mouse. Very refreshing, too, it was to see the little flower-gardens in front of the houses, with their blooming roses, and climbing vines, and orange trees with their golden fruit; and even hedges of roses, myrtles, aloes, and cactuses blooming profusely, and filling the pure atmosphere with their delicious fragrance; and to walk in the grateful shade of the long rows of venerable oaks, poplars, and pines that line the sides of the principal avenues.

They found, also, that the town almost covered the plot of ground extending from the beach southward to the almost perpendicular sides of Table Mountain; that the broad streets intersected each other at right angles; that some of them were threaded with canals, as in Holland; that most of them were destitute of sidewalks, and many of them without any pavements; and that the upper part of the town, near the mountain, is watered by a sprightly stream that issues from the upland on the east, and finds its way into Table Bay, at Cape Town; the banks of which are the resort of hosts of laundresses. They were gratified to find that there were numerous walks and drives in and around the town, of the most inviting character, and in the midst of beautiful scenery; especially over the macadamized road that leads eastward to Simon's Bay, amid corn-fields, orchards, gardens, and vineyards, shadowed overhead with stately aspens, darkly-waving pines, and majestic oaks, along the base of the Devil's Peak, with its cloud-capped summit, to the little village of Rondebosch, and the charming villas of Wynberg, a spot full of beauty, and enjoying a most delightful temperature of the atmosphere, the favored resort of the citizens of Cape Town, from which it is distant about seven or eight miles; and that gardens and pleasure-grounds, glittering with the graceful foliage of the Protea Argentea (silver tree), extended around the town, indicative of wealth, pleasure, and refinement. Their attention was particularly directed to the noble square, or parade-ground, called the "Heere Gracht," covering several acres of ground, in the midst of which stands the handsome structure, called the "Commercial Rooms," and the far-famed library of the Cape.

Here, under the noble avenues of pines, with their foliage of deepest green, sheltering from the burning rays of an almost tropical sun, troops of gay pedestrians might be seen enjoying the balmy atmosphere, and luxuriating in the midst of the grand and inspiring scenery. Every thing seemed to conspire to arrest their attention, and to furnish them with pleasing topics of thought and conversation.

While they found so much that was strange and peculiar, they also found that, even there, the gospel of the Lord Jesus Christ had shed its hallowed influence over Africans and Asiatics, as well as the boors and the British. Mr. Bertram had been furnished with letters of introduction to several of the servants of God who had made the Cape their home. Immediately on his arrival, he sought out these worthy men, and was most heartily welcomed to the southern hemisphere. He found himself very speedily at home in the society of that venerable man of God, the Rev. JOHN PHILIP, D.D., who, since 1829, had occupied the position of superintendent of the London Missionary Society's operations in Southern Africa, the tidings of whose recent decease have been received with so much sorrow by the Christian world. The Rev. JOHN C. BROWN, also, the minister of Union Chapel (Congregational), formerly of St. Petersburgh, Russia, the grandson of the renowned

John Brown, of Haddington, Scotland, whose visit to America, in 1836, will be remembered with pleasure by all who formed an acquaintance with him, and who has subsequently resided at Cape Town, as the assistant of Dr. Philip, gave him a cordial greeting. But from none did he find a more warm and brotherly reception than from the Rev. GEORGE MORGAN, of the Scottish Church, pastor of St. Andrew's, Somerset Road, who from the first deeply interested himself in the peculiar mission of Mr. Bertram, and continued to manifest the same untiring interest to the last moment of his stay at the Cape. Through the kind offices of these and other Christian friends, to whom he was introduced, among whom the name of the excellent and learned JAMES ADAMSON, D.D., deserves special mention, Mr. Bertram was soon provided with agreeable lodgings at the Cape, and encouraged in his plans for missionary service.

On the morning of the first Sabbath day after his arrival, he went down to the beach, to go on board the Luna, and preach to his former shipmates, agreeably to his appointment on leaving them to go ashore. He found Captain Carmichael waiting for him with his boat, and glad to receive him on board. To his surprise he found, on reaching the vessel, that the deck was almost covered with seamen, who had come from other vessels in the harbor to hear a sermon from the missionary.

On inquiry, he was told that all this was the work of "Jimmy Watt." Jimmy was an uneducated Scotch carpenter, who had resided at Cape Town about fifteen or twenty years, and, during all this time, had untiringly cared, without compensation, for the religious welfare of the thousands of seamen who had visited the port. Having furnished himself with a small boat, he was wont, on the morning of the Sabbath, when the weather would permit, to take with him a bundle of religious tracts, and row out into the anchorage, where not a few vessels were always to be found, and visit as many of them as he could, distributing his tracts to the seamen, and dropping a word or two of good advice to each of them, as opportunity offered. If at any time he could obtain from one of the shipmasters the privilege of a public gathering on the Sabbath for a sermon, he would endeavor to prevail upon some one of the ministers of the place, or missionaries who might be stopping there for a few days or weeks, to accompany him in his little boat to the Bethel, and give a sermon to the sailors, whom he took good care to invite from all the vessels in the harbor. He had thus gained the good-will of the mariners, and accomplished no small amount of spiritual good.

As soon as Jimmy Watt learned of the appointment on board of the Luna, he was on the alert, and spread the information among all the seamen at the port, with an invitation to attend the service on Sabbath morning. Nor had the captain of the Luna been idle. Between them both, a large congregation had been gathered, to whom Mr. Bertram proclaimed the message of salvation. Several of the shipmasters also had come to hear him, to whom he was introduced after the services were concluded. One of them pointed to his vessel, and said, "There, Mr. Bertram, is my ship." "A fine, large vessel," he replied; "how long do you remain in port?" "Two or three weeks, perhaps," was the answer. "Well, then," he asked again, "can't I preach on board your ship next Sabbath day?" "Certainly, Mr. Bertram," was the quick response; "I shall be most happy to have you come and preach on board, and I'll take care to see that every thing is ready for you." Accordingly, on the following Sabbath he went, and found a still larger congregation than on the previous occasion. Sabbath after Sabbath he went and preached, while the number of his hearers was continually increasing.

The work, into which he had thus been providentially directed, began also to attract the attention of the numerous Christian people of the town. They looked upon his coming as a call of God, to lead them to do something for the hundreds and thousands of seamen who resorted to that port. They held a preliminary meeting, and then a second more general meeting, at which it was determined to secure a sufficient salary, and engage Mr. Bertram to labor as the seamen's chaplain at Cape Town. With this arrangement Mr. Bertram was satisfied, although it was not just the thing that had brought him from Scotland; but, as the hand of God was so plainly in it, he could not as yet withdraw from it.

Just, however, as he was entering fully into his work, he was laid aside for a time by a severe disorder in one of his knees, during which period he received the utmost attention from his friend, Rev. George Morgan. By the kind and generous services of Dr. Bickersteth, under God's blessing, he obtained, after a short season of pain, entire relief, and resumed his labors.

Another sphere of usefulness was presently opened to him. One of the brethren of the Baptist persuasion called upon him on a Sabbath morning, to direct his attention to a work in which he himself, full of zeal and devotion, had for some time been employed. "I have heard," said he, "of your preaching among the seamen in the harbor, and it has given me great joy. It is needed very much. But I want you to come down this afternoon and preach to the prisoners, who are in still greater need, if possible. We have a snug little chapel within the prison walls, where you can be accommodated with a pretty large congregation; for the prison is quite full, principally, too, of seamen, who have committed some depredation, or other enormity, on ship-board. I myself go down at times and read to them a portion of God's word, and sometimes venture upon a few remarks. But you can be of far greater service to them, and I hope that you will consent to go down and preach to them this P.M. at three o'clock." Mr. Bertram consented to go, after preaching to the sailors in the morning.

A scene of peculiar interest was presented in the afternoon, when he went down to the prison. The brother who had invited him informed the keeper of the object of their coming, by whose direction the turnkey opened the cells, and marched the inmates into the chapel. But such an uncouth, disorderly, and unmannerly assembly he had never before addressed or seen. They seemed to have been the victims of long-continued dissipation, and to have indulged in all manner of ungodliness. One or two of them had even been arraigned for murder. It was with some instinctive shudderings that he saw the key turned upon himself and attendant, and felt that he was completely at the mercy of these unprincipled creatures.

But without delay he addressed himself to his work. As for reducing them to any kind of order, it seemed utterly impossible. They were noisy, rough, and profane, jostling each other about as if determined to prevent the missionary's object, and to produce as much confusion and disturbance as possible. It seemed to be a hopeless task to undertake to gain the attention of such a rude and ungodly assembly. It was like casting "pearls before swine." Yet, in the strength of the Lord, he determined to make the trial.

The brother, who had introduced him, commenced the service by giving out a hymn, which they two sang alone as well as they could. Mr. Bertram followed with prayer and a portion of Scripture. Still, the disturbance ceased not; and the irreverence of the audience was unblushing and shocking, so much so as almost to compel the missionary to abandon the attempt in despair. However, he resolved to go through with the service, if possible, and look to God to bring his unmanageable hearers into something like subjection.

Among this singular audience, the eye of the speaker had caught sight of one, a tall, muscular, lion-hearted fellow, with large whiskers and a brazen face, who seemed to be the ringleader in all this mischief. Having taken his text, Mr. Bertram endeavored to bring the burning truth of God's word to bear particularly and pointedly on this hardened creature, while the disturbance still continued. At length, "the strong man armed" was seen to bow his head, as one crest-fallen and ashamed. When that head was again lifted up, it was evident that the fountains of feeling had been reached, for the tears had been coursing each other down his cheeks. The tender sympathy began to spread, and one and another to preserve something like respectful silence, so that the service was concluded with much more decency and propriety than was observed at the commencement.

Encouraged by the success attendant upon this first effort, Mr. Bertram resolved to preach to them again, and to repeat his visits from Sabbath to Sabbath, if the way should be open. On the following Sabbath he succeeded still better, and had a comparatively sedate audience. An opportunity also presented itself for a weekly sermon at the hospital; so that he soon had as much work on his hands as he could well manage. Every Sabbath he preached in the morning to the sailors, in the afternoon to the prisoners, and at five o'clock in the afternoon to the poor, diseased inmates of the hospital. It was among some of the most degraded, criminal, and wretched of the pretenders to civilization that he was thus called to labor; nor did he shrink from it, or sigh for a more elevated class of hearers. It was for such as these that Jesus had died; and none, more than they, could profit by the purchase of the Redeemer's blood; and surely none could be found who more needed the benefits of that purchase. The meek and lowly Saviour, who came to seek and save that which was lost, and whom none heard so gladly as the common people, the poor, the wretched, and the outcast, was pleased to stand by His feeble servant, and strengthen him for his self-denying and arduous work. And never did that servant more habitually feel that he was walking in the footsteps of the God-man, the great pioneer in the work of missions to the perishing.

Not many weeks after the introduction of these services among the prisoners, the turnkey came up, on a Monday morning, to the lodgings of Mr. Bertram, and desired him to go down speedily to the prison, as his help was very much needed. A strange occurrence had taken place. "Why, sir," said the turnkey, "when we took the breakfast to the prisoners this morning, instead of being accosted with profane jesting, and blasphemous oaths, as usual, several of them appeared to be in the greatest distress, and begged us, for God's sake, to bring them Bibles." It was even so. A work of grace had commenced among these vile and abandoned sinners. God had blessed the word to their conviction; and now, as the missionary came to instruct and comfort them in their distress, they accosted him with the cry that was heard in the prison at Philippi, "What must I do to be saved?"

A short time after this, as Mr. Bertram was coming out of the door of a stationer's shop, he perceived two seamen, in decent apparel, and of orderly conduct, who appeared to recognize him, and to be desirous of accosting him. Going up to them pleasantly, he said, "Do you know me, men? I don't recollect to have seen either of you before." "Oh! yes," they replied, "we know you well. We belonged to your congregation in the prison, and are glad that we ever heard you." "But," as one of them looked at the other, he said, "I could not have believed that such a hard heart as mine would ever have been softened." "Nor I mine, either," responded the other. "I think," they continued, "that we were all softened. As for us, ever since we heard you preach, we have been determined to lead new lives, and try to save our souls and serve God. We have been discharged from prison, and have shipped on board that vessel that you see out there in the bay. We leave this afternoon, and would be glad if you could give us some religious tracts to read on the voyage." He took them to his lodgings, and gave them instruction in the way of life, with some suitable advice for their conduct at sea. He selected for them several tracts, and, bidding them farewell, he charged them to cleave with full purpose of heart to the Lord, and acknowledge Him in all their ways.

Another incident may be related, in this connection, bearing upon Mr. Bertram's usefulness in these prison ministrations. Among the poor creatures under arrest for crime, and confined in the jail, was a poor Hottentot, charged with murder. Having observed, in his visits to the prison, an appearance of deep anxiety and distress in the countenance of the criminal, he learned from the turnkey the nature of the accusation with which he was charged. But as he was unable to address him in the Dutch-Totty dialect, in use by these creatures, he called upon the Rev. George Morgan, who kindly consented to act as interpreter, and accompanied him to the prison. By the inquiries of Mr. Morgan, as well as his own through Mr. Morgan, he learned that the poor Hottentot could give no account of the matter with which he was charged; that, at the time when the man was killed, a mistake had been made in dealing out on the farm the spirit-rations, brandy having been substituted for the usual rations of Cape wine; and that, in consequence, the two men had become deeply intoxicated; that in this state they had first wrestled, and then quarreled; and the Hottentot, being at first brought down by his antagonist, had recovered his footing, and catching up a piece of a plowshare, had in turn prostrated with it the man, who thereby had lost his life.

On the trial, it was fully proved that the Hottentot had killed his companion with the dangerous instrument, and no defense was made. As it was about to go to the jury, and the attorney-general had risen to sum up the case on the part of the government, Mr. Bertram, who had been anxious to communicate what he knew, sought an opportunity of getting the ear of the distinguished attorney; who thereupon called the attention of the court to the fact that a reverend gentleman was present who had visited the prisoner officially, and who could present some mitigating considerations, which he briefly related. His Honor, the judge, immediately observed, that if it could be proved that the man had thus been surprised into a state of intoxication, it would take away all evidence of a murderous intention. Inquiry was then made, whether there was any one present who could testify to the facts respecting the liquor. A stranger rose in the court-room, and declared that he was ready to testify. After his examination, the case went to the jury, who returned a verdict of *manslaughter*, and the man was sentenced to three years' hard labor on the roads. As the court adjourned, Mr. Bertram was universally congratulated by several distinguished citizens, as having had the happiness of saving the life of the poor Hottentot, who, but for him, would have been found guilty of murder, and executed.

In the midst of such useful services to humanity, and in the prosecution of his spiritual labors among the sailors, the sick, and the prisoners, Mr. Bertram's time glided pleasantly along. He saw the fruit of his services, thanked God, and took courage.

CHAPTER III.

LABORS AT SALDANHA BAY.

A NEW and remarkable scene, in the history of Mr. Bertram, now opens before us. While pursuing his self-denying and useful exertions at the Cape, he resolved to make an excursion some sixty miles to the north. A large number of vessels had called at Table Bay, and procured permission of the government to proceed to Saldanha Bay, and take in a cargo of guano. In addition to their crews, each vessel also shipped some ten or twelve coolies, or Malays, to serve them in getting in their cargoes. The business held out a prospect of large pecuniary returns, and was, of course, much talked of in the commercial circles at Cape Town. It was ascertained that from one hundred and fifty to two hundred vessels, some of them of one thousand tons burden, were anchored in Saldanha Bay, and that a population, most heterogeneous, of nearly or quite two thousand souls, were congregated in the bay.

The hearts of God's people at the Cape were moved, at the thought of the heathenish condition in which this large number of souls were living for weeks and months, without the ordinances of religion, with no one to give them spiritual consolations in sickness, none to point the dying to the Lamb of God, and none to perform the services of religion at the burial of the dead. Mr. Bertram was so much affected by these considerations, as to determine to go down, if possible, to Saldanha Bay for a short time, and do something for the souls of this neglected and destitute population. On making known his intentions to his friends at the Cape, he was encouraged to proceed. The Rev. John C. Brown, of Union Chapel, in particular, took a very deep interest in the matter. As soon as he heard of it, he came to Mr. Bertram, and said, "Go, my brother, in the name of the Lord; and may Jacob's God go with you." He furnished him also with the means of purchasing an overcoat, for protection from the storms to which he might be exposed, in a place where there were none but canvas tenements to shelter him. His kindness in this particular, as in many others, is, and ever will be, held in grateful remembrance.

The ship "Ward Chipman," of St. John's, New Brunswick, commanded by Captain Aymers, a Scotchman, was then lying in Table Bay, expecting to sail in a few days for Saldanha. Mr. Bertram sought him out, and made known to him his desire to procure a passage on board his ship. The captain was a man of a large heart, and very readily offered the missionary a passage, and the attentions of the steward of the ship, during all his continuance at Saldanha Bay, without any compensation. The necessary arrangements having been made on shore, Mr. Bertram bade farewell to his family and friends, and embarked on board the "Ward Chipman," on a Wednesday evening, in the latter part of April, 1845.

Saldanha Bay is a "magnificent haven" on the southwest coast of Africa, about sixty miles north of Table Bay, in lat. 32° 54′ south. It was discovered by the Portuguese, not long after the discovery, in 1487, of the "Capo de Boa Esperance," or Cape of Good Hope, and called "Saldanha," after a town of that name, in the northwest of Spain, in the province of Leon, probably the birthplace of some of the discoverers.

It was first visited, so far as we can now learn, in the summer of 1620, a few months before the landing of the Pilgrims on the shores of New England. Two East India merchantmen, on their outward voyage, put in at this bay, and their commanders, Fitzherbert and Shillinge, issued a proclamation, dated "Bay of Saldanha, 3d July, 1620," in which they claimed the territory for King James I. No attempts were made, either then or subsequently, to colonize the country by the subjects of the King of Great Britain. In the journals of Dr. Van Riebeck, the first Dutch Governor of the Cape Colony, frequent mention is made of the natives that came from Saldanha Bay. One of the vessels belonging to the Dutch, called the "Good Hope," was employed in 1652 in exploring expeditions to Saldanha Bay, and in bringing thence, for the use of the colonists, supplies of penguins and sea-birds' eggs, which were there found in great abundance.

John Baptist Tavernier, of Paris, on his return from the East Indies, in 1649, passed a few days among the natives at the Cape, where the ship obtained a great supply of birds' eggs, "as big as goose eggs." He represents these birds as a sort of goose, and says, "They breed in such great quantities in the country, that in a bay, about eighteen leagues from the Cape, you may knock them on the head with a stick." Commodore Roggewein, who visited this region in 1733, says, that "at the distance of about eighteen leagues from the Cape, there is another port, called the Bay of Saldeney, which is, in all respects, an infinitely better harbor than that of the Cape, except one, and that is, in point of water." The distance accords with the description of Tavernier, and shows that the latter had reference to this bay, when he spoke of it as the resort of innumerable birds. In the journal of Governor

Zacharias Wagenaar, the successor of Van Riebeck at the Cape, appears the following memorandum, under date of February 17, 1666: "Sent the 'Crowned Herring' to Saldanha Bay, to fetch a load of sea-birds' dung for our gardens."

The colony of the Cape of Good Hope was surrendered to the forces of Great Britain, under the command of General Craig, September 16th, 1795. But the Dutch, not willing to relinquish a naval post of so much importance, of which they had retained possession since 1652, fitted out an expedition, under Admiral Lucas, consisting of two sixty-fours, one fifty-four, four frigates, and a sloop, which arrived safely, and cast anchor in Saldanha Bay, August 2d, 1796. While they were refitting the vessels, and refreshing the crews and marines after their long voyage, a British fleet, under the command of Admiral Elphinstone, consisting of two seventy-fours, five sixty-fours, one fifty, and six other vessels came to anchor within gun-shot of the Dutch fleet; and, knowing how much superior his own force was to that of the blockaded squadron, the British admiral sent a written summons for the surrender of Admiral Lucas's command. Reasonable terms of capitulation having been submitted, the latter surrendered his whole fleet without the firing of a gun. The bay has thus acquired a considerable historical importance.

But a few years since it acquired a still greater, and far more substantial, importance, by reason of the guano traffic, to which allusion has already been made. The fertilizing properties of the excrements of birds seem to have been known by the second governor of the Cape, nearly two hundred years since. But it is only within these twelve or fifteen years that scientific agriculture has brought fully to light the valuable qualities of these ammonial deposits, and created a demand for the article. During a long succession of ages, a considerable number of the rocky and uninhabited islands on the coasts of Africa and South America, particularly in the neighborhood of the two capes, at the southern extremities of the two continents, and along the shores of Peru and Bolivia, have been the resort of immense numbers of the singular water-fowl, known as the penguin, or pinguin, and others of like habits.

Ferdinand Magellan, who sailed along the Atlantic coast of Patagonia in 1519, "met with a couple of islands so full of seals and penguins, that, in an hour's space, they could have laden all the five ships." He describes them as "a black, unwieldy fowl, extremely fat, covered over with a sort of down, instead of feathers, and armed with a bill like a raven's." These islands have since been known as "the Great and Little Penguins." They were visited also by the Dutch commander

De Weert, in 1599, who says, that such was the multitude of penguins, "they might have furnished twenty-five ships with them;" and that "they took above nine hundred in two hours' time." He gives a minute description of them, and says, that, when full grown, they weigh from twelve to sixteen pounds; that they are black upon the back, and white on the under parts, having also a white ring around the neck, having a skin like a sea-dog's, and as thick as the skin of a wild boar; that their bill is as long as a raven's, but not as crooked; that their necks are short and thick, and their body as long as a goose's, but not so big. He says that, instead of wings, they have two fins hanging down, and covered with feathers, with which they swim with great ease.

Laval, on his voyage to the East Indies, in 1601, landed at Annabon, an island about one hundred miles south of the line, in the Atlantic, and discovered in the neighborhood a small rocky island, bare of vegetation, but so covered with penguins, that no one could walk anywhere without treading upon their eggs. Commodore Beaulieu, who visited the Cape of Good Hope in 1620, describes an island about two leagues north of Table Bay, a large league in circumference, on which great numbers of penguins were found. Captain Funnel, in 1706, calls it, "Penguin Island," and says, that it takes its name from a vast number of birds, about the bigness of a wild duck, with a sharp bill, and feet like a duck, having no wings, but stumps only, with which they fly not, but flutter, called penguins.

The name is by some supposed to have been derived from the Latin word *pinguis*, fat. Others derive the word from a term in the old British language, signifying *whiteness*, because of their white heads. But Dr. Harris, in his Bibliotheca of Travels, affirms, that the name was given them by the aborigines.

The congregation of these birds, for ages, in countless generations and immense numbers, on some isolated rock, undisturbed by human visitants, has resulted in the vast deposits of the fertilizing substance to which the name *guano* has been affixed, and which, at the time of Mr. Bertram's visit, was found in such quantity at Saldanha Bay. The name is of Peruvian origin. In that tongue, *huano*, pronounced by the Spaniards *guano*, means *dung*. The Peruvians have long been acquainted with the agricultural virtue of this substance. Vast stores of this bird's dung have been found for ages on the Chincha Islands, near the fourteenth parallel of south latitude, three rocky protuberances from the sea, of five or six miles' circuit, and about ten miles from the main land. Here it was found, at the commencement of the traffic, in a perfect state of preservation, by reason of the infrequency of rains on that coast, and of the average depth of one hundred feet, in some places two hundred. Humboldt, in 1804, called attention to this deposit, and referred to its enriching qualities. The great guano port of Peru is Iquique. The Peruvians have a proverb, "Huano, though no saint, works miracles;" referring to the wonderfully-fertilizing power of this article.

At the commencement of this trade, the principal source of traffic on the coast of Africa was a small island, called Icheboe, farther to the north, in the twenty-sixth degree of south latitude; but the demand soon exhausted the supply, and the attention of the trade was now directed to the spot whither Mr. Bertram was bound.

The "Ward Chipman" proceeded on her way, and arrived off the bay about ten o'clock in the evening of Thursday. The night was dark, and the captain, not being acquainted with the channel, attempted to enter on the wrong side of the island, that divides the mouth into two nearly equal parts. Presently the breakers were seen within a few yards, and the position of the ship became quite perilous. The main anchor was speedily dropped, and the vessel stayed. As soon as it was known in the harbor, six and twenty boats were manned by the shipmasters and their men, by whose timely and powerful aid, the vessel was towed, with the loss of her anchor, and with no further injury, to a safe and quiet anchorage within the land-locked harbor.

The morning light revealed the hidden dangers of the previous evening, and the peculiarities of the scenery in the midst of which they had reposed during the night. The dark olive-tint of the water, approaching almost to black, indicated, to some extent, the character of the traffic which was prosecuted on its surface. A more beautiful and safe haven for ships, they had seldom, if ever, seen. It seemed to be of several leagues in circumference, capable of containing the whole navy of Great Britain, and almost entirely shut in by the land, which rose on nearly every hand in gentle swells, and verdant plains, and was covered with a prolific vegetation. Immediately in front, toward the sea, and occupying a large portion of the strait, by which the bay was entered, appeared a small island, of singular aspect, called Maleasen, Malagasen, or, more commonly, "Malagas Island." The bay was dotted in every direction with merchant-vessels of all descriptions, and hundreds of yawls, barges, and freight-boats were attached to the ships, or moving quietly over the smooth surface of the bay.

In the center of the island was a flag-staff, from which lines extended in every direction to the water's edge. On nearer inspection, it was found that the soil with which the island was covered, was a vast bed of guano, some twenty or thirty feet in depth, that had been accumulating for ages, and which was now in the process of exportation to the four quarters of the globe. The lines from the flag-staff were designed to mark out, like the divisions of a plum-cake, to the crew of each vessel, the particular portion which they might claim as their own. At the water's edge was a jetty, or wharf, near which were seen scaffoldings, designed to facilitate the transportation of the various "diggings" to the boats; while all over the island the canvas huts and tents of the workmen, formed of sails and tarpaulins, thrown over spars and yards from the vessels, gave evidence of a numerous population. Gay banners and streamers were floating over these nautical encampments, inscribed with some fanciful appellation, indicating the vessel or country to which the occupants belonged, or showing some of the eccentricities of seamen; such as "Sheerness," "Wapping," "London Docks," etc.

The spectator was at once reminded of the resemblance of the whole scene to a country fair, such, particularly, as are held every August at "Donnybrook," in the county of Dublin, where for six days the usquebaugh circulates most freely, and the shillalah flourishes in the air, giving weight and force to the brilliant points of Irish wit and argument. That Scripture, whicn says, "Wheresoever the carcass is, there will the eagles be gathered together," was strikingly fulfilled at Malagas Island. The opportunity of trading with such an assemblage, as were there congregated for weeks, could not be resisted by the suttlers and grog-sellers at the Cape, who had flocked hither to share in the golden harvest, and pitched their tents along the shores of the bay. They found a ready market for their vile compounds of wine, rum, brandy, and other death-dealing liquors ; and frequent, as well as violent, were the scenes of riot and blood-letting, with which this woeful traffic was followed. The poor sea-fowl, whose domain had thus summarily and unceremoniously been invaded, had fled to other rocky points in and along the bay, where they seemed to be taking counsel as to the best means of regaining their time-honored territory.

Such was the spectacle that presented itself to the eye of Mr. Bertram, on the morning after his arrival. After breakfast, he was put ashore on the main land, in the vicinity of a large cave formed by overhanging rocks. This natural habitation had been appropriated by an old Hibernian, of the sons of Æsculapius, a stout, overgrown, and somewhat venerable personage, who had converted the interior of his primitive habitation into a rude resemblance of an apothecary's shop, with mysterious-looking bottles and vials ranged around, in number sufficient to kill or cure all who might wish to avail themselves of his wondrous pharmaceutic lore, and unrivaled skill in the treatment of all the ills to which the flesh of man is subject. There, ensconced in his mysterious habitation, that served him as office, parlor, ante-chamber, dormitory, and kitchen, he sagely gave out, that he would undertake the wholesale cure of broken bones and bleeding wounds, for the moderate sum of five pounds a ship. Nor was he unemployed. The disorderly and dissipated manner in which a large portion of the sailors and laborers lived; the exposures to which they were constantly subjected; the large potations of intoxicating liquors with which they were furnished; the want of vegetable food; the constant use of salt provisions, and the overpowering effluvium of the guano itself, producing, by reason of the vast quantities of ammonia, inflammation and bleeding of the eyes and nostrils, served to bring into constant service the skill and the drugs of the old Irish doctor, and to test his power over such obstinate diseases as the dysentery, scurvy, and "redness of eyes."

At the time of Mr. Bertram's landing, a considerable number of the shipmasters were assembled about the "doctor's shop," apparently in earnest and anxious consultation. On inquiry, he learned enough to show him the hazardous nature of the mission, with which he had charged himself in coming to Saldanha Bay. The islanders, it appeared, were in a terrible state of insubordination and mutiny. The sailors, under the influence of frequent draughts of alcoholic compounds, had quarreled with the sable coolies from the Cape, and, in the terrible excitement of rage and intoxication, had belabored them with furious blows, and then driven them into the sea, where they would have been drowned but for the luggage-boats employed in transferring the guano to the ships, into which they were drawn out of the sea by the shipmasters, who had witnessed the mutiny. All business was in consequence suspended, and the most terrible scenes of drunkenness and insubordination ensued. In vain were all the efforts of the masters of the vessels to bring them into subjection. They were met with volleys of guano, assailed with the carcasses of penguins and gannets, and compelled to flee for their lives, and betake themselves to their boats. A second attempt to subdue the rioters by means of cutlasses and fire-arms, resulted in complete failure, only serving the more to exasperate both parties.

The shipmasters were now at their wit's ends. It was determined to hold a conference on shore, and consult on the best means of quelling the revolt. Something effectual was demanded, and that speedily, or they could not answer to the owners of the vessels for their failure in securing a cargo, and subjecting them to severe loss. As for unfurling their sails, and putting out to sea as they were, it was out of the question. At length it was determined to dispatch, over land, four of the most respectable shipmasters, to Cape Town, and solicit his excellency, Sir Peregrine Maitland, the governor of the colony, to send them a ship of war, to bring the mutineers to their senses and duty.

The land-route was circuitous, and much longer than by sea. Three or four days were occupied in the journey, assistance being afforded them by the Dutch farmers who occupied the interior. Several days, therefore, elapsed before any information or assistance could be procured from the Cape, during all which time the state of insubordination continued.

Mr. Bertram, being thus shut out from the great body of the seamen, whose spiritual welfare had brought him to Saldanha Bay, endeavored to employ his time with as much profit as the circumstances would permit. As the Sabbath was at hand, he desired to secure an opportunity for preaching. Learning that Captain Samson, of the ship "John Jordan," from Bristol, was a religious man, he made an arrangement with him to convert his ship into a Bethel. Quite a goodly number of the officers, and many of the seamen who were not compromised in the mutiny, assembled on the "John Jordan," at the appointed time, to whom he opened the treasures of God's word, and made known his commission as an ambassador of the Prince of Peace. At the pressing invitation of Captain Samson, whom he found to be in reality a man of God, he removed from the "Ward Chipman," and took up his quarters on the "John Jordan." The captain gave up to him his own cabin, and showed him every attention and kindness in his power, during the whole time of his sojourn at Saldanha Bay.

The delay, occasioned by the non-arrival of the aid expected from the Cape, gave Mr. Bertram frequent opportunities for exploring the shores of the bay. His early occupation had served to make him familiar with the vegetable creation. A passion for flowers had grown with his growth, and strengthened with his strength; and here, on this virgin soil, he found abundant means of gratifying it. Every day, after breakfast, the Jordan's boat was at his service, and he was put on the shore, to ramble off into "the bush," and meditate in the fields. Hour after hour he would ramble on for miles together, without the slightest interruption from any human being, and without any earthly witnesses of his footsteps, save an occasional monkey sporting on the rocks, and numerous birds, of most beautiful plumage. Nothing can exceed the splendor of the coloring—blue, green, yellow, scarlet, and crimson, alternating with the purest black and white—with which the feathered tribes are here adorned. To a lover of nature they present, with their infinite variety of song, a constant source of admiration.

Nor are the beauties of the vegetable world in Southern Africa less inviting and peculiar. "At every step we take," says Sir Cornwallis Harris, "what thousands and tens of thousands of gay flowers rear their lovely heads around us! Of a surety, the enthusiasm of the botanist has not painted the wonders of these regions in colors more brilliant than they deserve; for Africa is the mother of the most magnificent exotics that grace the green-houses of Europe. Turn where we will, some new plant discovers itself to the admiring gaze; and every barren rock being decorated with some large and strong blossom, it can be no exaggeration to compare the country to a botanical garden left in a state of nature. The regal protea (silver tree) here blossoms spontaneously on every side; the buzzing hosts of bees, beetles, and other parasites, by which its choicest sweets are surrounded, being often joined by the tiny humming-bird, herself scarcely larger than a butterfly, who perches on the edge of a broad flower, and darts her tubular tongue into the chalce."

"But the bulbous plants," adds the same author, "must be considered to form the most characteristic class; and in no region of the globe are they to be found so numerous, so varied, or so beautiful. To the brilliant and sweet-smelling ixia, and to the superb species of the iris (flower de luce), there is no end; the morell, the corn-flag (gladiolus), the amaryllis, the haemanthus, and pancratium, being countless as the sands upon the sea-shore. After the autumnal rains, their gaudy flowers, mixed with those of the brilliant orchidae, impart life and beauty, for a brief season, to the most sandy wastes, and, covering alike the meadows and the foot of the mountains, are succeeded by the graphalium, the xeranthemum, and a whole train of everlastings, which display their red, blue, or silky-white flowers, among a host of scented geraniums, flourishing like so many weeds. Even in the midst of stony deserts arise a variety of aloes and other fleshy plants, as, the stapelia, or carion-flower, with square, succulous, leafless stems, and flowers resembling star-fish. The brilliant mesanbryanthemum, or fig-marigold, extends to nearly three hundred species. But amid this gay and motley assemblage, the heaths, whether in number or beauty, stand confessedly unrivaled. Nature has extended that elegant shrub to almost every soil and situation—the marsh, the river-brink, the richest loam, and the barest rural cliff, being alike

'Empurpled with the heather's dye.'

Upward of three hundred and fifty distinct species exist; nor is the form of their flowers less diversified than are their varied hues. Cup-shaped, globular, and bell-shaped; some exhibit the figure of a cone; others that of a cylinder; some are contracted at the base, others in the middle; and still more are bulged out like the mouth of a trumpet. While many are smooth and glossy, some are covered with down, and others, again, are incrusted with mucilage. Red, in every variety of depth and shade, from blush to the brightest crimson, is their prevailing complexion; but green, yellow, and purple are scarcely less abundant, and blue is almost the only color whose absence can be remarked."

Such are the beauties of the vegetable creation in the southern portion of that mysterious continent, whose vast interior yet remains to be explored by civilized man, and to the richness and gorgeousness of whose productions no other portion of the world can scarcely afford a parallel.

The season of the year in which these rural walks of Mr. Bertram were prosecuted, was not the most favorable for the development of all these floral beauties. The heats of summer had passed, and the period of vegetable repose was drawing on. The April of that hemisphere, it will be remembered, answers to our October, and it was near the close of the month when he arrived. But still he saw enough, especially in the endless varieties and quantities of the bulbous tribes, to give him some conception of what the scene must be in the early spring, August and September. There he found plants, which in his youth he had cultivated in the green-house, and treated as precious exotics, growing wild, and in the greatest abundance.

It was not his fortune to come in sight of any of the mighty beasts of prey with which the interior abounds, and which sometimes show themselves on the coast. Many of the large African bullocks, brought in by the Dutch boors, or farmers, were slaughtered on the shore for the use of the ships, by the butchers who had been attracted to the spot, and whose tents were pitched on the main land. On one occasion, as Mr. Bertram was preparing to take his morning walk, one of these sons of slaughter said to him, "I would advise you not to go very far into the bushes this morning, as the lions have been roaring about our tents all night. We have killed so many cattle that they have been drawn here by the scent of blood." With some hesitation, and in the exercise of a good degree of cautiousness, he however concluded to go, but met with no other harm than a good scaring at a sudden rustling in the bushes, which proved to be only a winged lion, or something else that takes to itself wings, and flies away.

The vast quantities of arable land, exceedingly fertile, and entirely unoccupied, capable of producing immense crops of grains and other vegetables, arrested his attention, and turned his thoughts to the starving millions of Europe, and especially of Scotland and Ireland, who know not how to eke out a subsistence from day to day. He could not but think, what a blessing it would be to both hemispheres, if a few thousands of the hardy sons of toil would emigrate to the rich and unoccupied lands of Southern Africa, and begin to develop the immense but hidden resources of that luxuriant continent. Millions, who at home have not so much as a small cabbage-garden, might there possess their broad acres of meadow and of grain, with all the vegetable products that are desirable for man's comfort on earth. Sometimes, in these rambles, he would amuse his idle hours by fancying himself a planter. "Here," he would say, as his eye rested on a spacious level rock, surrounded by beautiful meadows—"here would be just the spot to build my house; here I would have my garden; there my barns, there the lawn, and here the park. What a magnificent site it would be!"

While he was thus amusing himself with these daily recreations, and airy castles, it came into his mind that this was not just the thing that brought him to Saldanha Bay. "All this," he said to himself, "is very fine; but what sort of a missionary am I? When I was at home in Great Britain, I thought that I could go and preach Christ even to the cannibals. Like the great Apostle to the Gentiles, I could say, 'Neither count I my life dear unto myself, so that I might finish my course with joy, and the ministry which I have received of the Lord Jesus, to testify the Gospel of the grace of God,' even among the most degraded and abandoned of the heathen world. But now that I have come in sight of danger, what a cowardly missionary I prove to be! I came to this bay for the very purpose of preaching to these seamen on Malagas Island, and now I have not courage enough to show my face among them!" The example of the noble John Williams, who laid down his life among the cannibals of the South Sea Islands, came to his mind; and he thought of other holy missionaries, who had jeoparded their lives even unto death in carrying the Gospel to the perishing; and he was mortified and humbled at his own pusillanimity.

Thus brought, as it were, to his senses, and to a proper conception of the nature and requirements of his mission, he sought a retired place among the rocks, and confessed, with a broken heart, to his Saviour, the unbelief and sinful fear by which he had been actuated, sought forgiveness at the feet of his Lord and Master, and solemnly vowed before God, that, life and health permitting, he would go on the following Sabbath to Malagas Island, and preach, even if he should die for it, to the mutineers.

At three o'clock, the hour when the Jordan's boat came daily to the shore to take him on board to dine, he returned to the ship. At the dinner-table, he said to the captain, "Captain Samson! I wish to ask a favor of you." "Very well, what is it?" "I want you to take me in your boat next Sabbath morning to the island, that I may preach there."

The captain was taken wholly by surprise. Suppressing for a few moments his amazement, as he stared at Mr. Bertram, he at length said, "What, sir! are you mad? You do n't catch me doing so foolish a thing as to take you up to the island among those men. They would only desecrate the service, and perhaps take your life."

"But what then?" was the reply of Mr. Bertram; "will you leave these men under the influence of the devil, and make no effort for their improvement? What is to make them better, if we refuse to carry the Gospel among them?" "Well," responded the captain, "say what you will, I 'll never take you up to the island." The captain was evidently nettled for once; but it was only for once. The matter was dropped for the present.

Just then a ship of war hove in sight, which proved to be one of Her Majesty's vessels that had been lying at Simon's Bay, or False Bay, as it was formerly called, on the eastern side of the peninsula, that terminates in the Cape of Good Hope, on the west side of which Cape Town is built; which vessel had been ordered to Saldanha Bay to quell the mutiny. The rioters had given themselves up to gluttony and drunkenness. Day after day they had kept up their horrid frolic, until they had exhausted the stores on the island. Then they had crossed over to the mainland, and possessed themselves of the contents of some of the suttlers' shanties, with which they had returned, and recommenced their terrible carousing.

In the midst of their bacchanalian revel, they were brought to their senses by the presence of an armed detachment of marines from the ship of war, who had effected a landing from their boats with the greatest order and dispatch. They saw at once that resistance was useless; and, when ordered by the commander of the frigate to acknowledge their wickedness, and sue for mercy, or he would open his ports upon them, and blow them to pieces, they begged, in the most abject manner, that he would let them off this time, and promised to go to work like honest men, and never again be guilty of such wicked conduct.

The result was very gratifying to the officers of the man-of-war, and to the shipmasters. Congratulations were exchanged from one to another, and the commander of the armed vessel received on board the various ships with every testimonial of gratitude. He assured them all, that the rebellion was at an end; that the rioters were completely humbled, had manifested the greatest sorrow for their disorderly and criminal conduct, and given him the utmost assurance, that they would all quietly and submissively return to duty; that they might now take in their cargoes with all dispatch, and ere long heave anchor, unfurl their sails, and bend their course homeward.

It was not in the power of the commander to make any stay in the harbor. He had been ordered to the western coast of Africa, on a cruise, to watch the slave ships, and break up their piratical traffic. He could not, therefore, remain in port any longer, after he had fulfilled his commission in coming to Malagas Island. His vessel was soon again under way, and, with a favoring breeze, pursuing her course toward the north.

But, no sooner had the vessel disappeared, than, relieved of their fears, the revelers broke over all restraint, and returned to their former state of insubordination. They became more and ore infatuated and maddened; they formed parties among themselves according to the port or ships to which they belonged; they chose ringleaders, calling them by the names of wild beasts, as they really seemed to be. To one they gave the name Lion; to another, the name Bear; to another, Tiger, and the like. All hope of a compromise was entirely taken away, and the shipmasters were completely at their wit's end.

Mr. Bertram had watched the progress of the whole affair with the deepest interest; and, when he saw the utter failure of the remedy devised by the wrath of man, he assuredly gathered, that the Lord was calling him to put in practice the purpose that he had formed, and fulfill his solemn vow to God. He therefore renewed his application to Captain Samson, on the morning of the following Sabbath, and requested him to accompany the missionary to the island, in his boat; but the captain was resolute. He would not be a party in such a rash expedition, nor would he risk the life of his friend among such a set of incarnate demons.

Among the vessels in port was the brig Hebe, of London, under the command of Captain Mosey. Mr. Bertram had formed an acquaintance with him at Cape Town, and learned from him that he had once made a profession of religion, and had "run well" for a season; but that on these long voyages he had got away from duty, and, falling into temptation at foreign ports, had suffered himself to be carried along with the tide of ungodliness, which he had not sufficient grace to stem and resist. He had, in consequence, become a wanderer from God, and a grievous, but not inveterate, backslider. He had manifested, in the apparent sorrow with which he had confessed all this to Mr. Bertram, that his conscience was yet tender; and so had led the missionary to think, that some traces of grace remained. When a soul has once been renewed by the Spirit, he can never again be as other men are. Let him wander ever so far, he will still have some clinging of heart, like the prodigal son, to his former experience, and be often saying to himself, "Oh that I were as in months past, as in the days when God preserved me, when His candle shined upon my head, and when by His light I walked through darkness!" He will now and then be saying—

"Where is the blessedness I knew,
When first I saw the Lord?
Where is the soul-refreshing view,
Of Jesus, and His word?

What peaceful hours I once enjoy'd!
How sweet their memory still!
But they have left an aching void,
The world can never fill."

Mr. Bertram, relying on this knowledge of the

case of his backsliding friend, went off to the Hebe, and found the captain standing on deck to receive him. "Captain Mosey!" he said, "I have come to beg a favor of you this morning." "What can I do for you, Mr. Bertram?" was the reply; "you know that I 'll do any thing and every thing that I can for you." "Yes, I know it," said Mr. Bertram, "and so I have come to ask you to take me up in your boat to the island, that I may preach the Gospel to those poor rebels there, this morning."

The request occasioned quite a struggle in the breast of Captain Mosey. After pacing the deck for a few moments, he turned, with moistened eyes, and a full heart, to the missionary, and said, "You know, Mr. Bertram, that I dare not take you up to the island. It was barely with my life that I escaped the other day. But come over to Captain Kerr's vessel with me, and we'll talk it over." So to Captain Kerr's ship, the "Fama," of London, they went, who, as soon as he saw them on deck, saluted them with "Good-morning, gentlemen; what has brought you here this morning!" "Why," said Captain Mosey, "here 's Mr. Bertram begging me to take him in my boat up to the island, to preach to those seamen." "What!" exclaimed Captain Kerr, "preach to those seamen! preach to those devils! preach to those *devils!*" "Yes," replied Captain Mosey, "and I think that he will not rest until we take him up." "What, to those devils! those infamous scoundrels?" responded Captain Kerr; "they ought to be hung, every devil of them. And are you going to take him up, Captain Mosey?" "Why," said Mosey, "if you will go, I 'll make one of the company." "But you know, Mosey," replied Kerr, "how they love me on the island, and how they treated me the last time that I was there! And where, if we go, are we to find a couple of oarsmen?" So, stepping to the hatchway, he shouted the name of one of the sailors; and the quick response, "Aye, aye, sir," was presently followed by his appearance on deck. "Come, my lad," said Kerr, "I want you to pull an oar to take Mr. Bertram to the island to preach to those devils there: what say you?" "Are you going, captain?" the man anxiously asked; "if you go, I 'll go, too." Another oarsman was obtained from Captain Mosey's brig, and presently they were pulling away for Malagas Island.

The morning was as lovely as can be conceived—just such a Sabbath as disposes the heart to peace and quietness, while it leads the soul away to the bowers of paradise, and impressively reminds the soul of that rest which remaineth to the people of God. Hardly a word was spoken, or the silence of the five adventurers interrupted, during the two miles and a half, at which distance the Hebe was moored from the island.

As the boat neared the landing-place, scores of the rioters hurried down to the jetty, or wharf, to see who dared approach their territories. A horrid sight these poor, infatuated creatures presented! Their clothes were almost torn from their backs, and hung about them in tatters. Hideous gashes, in some cases, and in others, blackened eyes, and dreadful bruises, gave evidence of the maddening fumes of dissipation by which they had, for days together, been driven to the extremes of brutal fury. Captains Kerr and Mosey sat almost stupefied, as they gazed on these hideous wretches. Nor was Mr. Bertram less moved with instinctive apprehension. He trusted not, however, in himself, but in the living God, and lifted his heart to the Almighty to nerve his soul for the hazardous enterprise.

Having fully committed himself to the protection and guidance of his Lord, he seized the ladder of ropes, as soon as the boat touched the jetty, and, pulling himself up, in a few moments he stood in the midst of the horrid crew. Singling out one, whom he took to be a ringleader, a tall, powerful, ferocious-looking fellow, apparently prepared for any deed of desperation, he went directly to him, gave him his right hand, and, with his left, tapped him on the shoulder, and said,

"Jack! do you know me?" "How should I know you, sir?" he muttered. "Well, well," replied Mr. Bertram, "I am a minister of Christ, and I have come to-day, in the name of the Lord, to preach among you the glorious Gospel of the blessed God." Then, pulling from his pocket a flag, with which he had furnished himself before leaving the vessel, he continued, "Do you see this, Jack? This is the battle-flag of the Cross, that I brought down with me from the Cape of Good Hope. I see that you have a flag-staff up there on the island. Now, my brave fellow, take this flag, and let me see how quick you can run it up to the mast-head." Turning to another savage-looking fellow, who stood by, he patted him also on the shoulder, and said to him, "That's a brave fellow, Jack; off and help him."

It was enough. The right chord was touched. Away they went, hurrahing, the whole of them, and in a few moments more the Bethel-flag was flying from the top of the flag-staff. The signal roused the whole island, and they flew from every tent and lounging-place, hundreds of them together, to know what was to pay now. The preacher planted himself on a pile of guano-bags, and began his brief arrangements for the service. But what a motley assemblage of human beings stood before him! They seemed to be the offscourings of every British port on earth, such as might well remind him of the hideous tenants of pandemonium itself.

They gazed mutually at each other in silence, a moment or two, and the missionary began: "Men! I have somewhat to say to you. What think ye, that the shipmasters down yonder in the bay said to me, when I told them that I was coming here this morning to preach the Gospel of Christ to you? Why, they told me that you were the greatest vagabonds under heaven; that you would desecrate the service of God, and take my life. But, my brave lads, I tell you that I am never afraid, under God, to trust my life in the hands of seamen. Now, men, if you will only listen to what I have to say to you, and take the good advice that I am about to give you, you will have an opportunity to-day of redeeming your lost character. Some of you, I dare say, were brought up in your tender years under the care of pious parents. Your godly fathers and mothers used to talk to you, no doubt, about your souls, and the things of God and heaven. They read to you, perhaps, the Holy Scriptures, and took you with them to the sanctuary of the Lord on the Sabbath day. Some serious impressions may have been made upon your minds by the good Spirit of God. You may remember the pious ministers whose sermons you heard in your boyhood, and under the sound of whose ministry you sat.

"But, ah! that was 'long, long ago.' You left the parental roof, and shipped for a foreign port; you were thrown into the company of ungodly men, by whose example, conversation, and raillery, you were led to shake off the impressions of early days; and by degrees you lost the remembrance of a father's counsel, a mother's prayers, your good minister's discourses, and those early impressions from the Lord. You were led into haunts of dissipation and vice, and gradually became hardened in sin, until you have arrived at your present pitch of iniquity.

"Think, O men! bethink yourselves of your early impressions, of the good advice of your parents, and the instructions of those Christian ministers; and let there be now a little serious reflection, while I preach to you, on Malagas Island, the glorious gospel of the blessed God. Some of you, I doubt not, are good singers. Your vocal powers are admirable. You can sing in your groggeries and merry-makings, but you never employ these powers for the glory of God. Perhaps there never was sung on Malagas Island a song of praise to God. Let us have the first song of praise to our Maker here this morning."

He had brought with him several seamen's hymn-books, which he now took from his pocket, and distributed among them, saying, "Here, men, are some pretty little hymn-books—hymns made for sailors. I brought them down from the Cape of Good Hope. Now I will give out one of the hymns. Captain Kerr"—(for the two captains had followed him)—"will pitch the tune, and let us all sing together, the hymn commencing with these words :

'O God of Bethel, by whose hand,
Thy people still are fed ;
Who through this weary pilgrimage,
Hast all our fathers led.'

Now, Captain Kerr, be so good as to pitch the tune. Come, my lads, strike in—sing all together : a long pull, a strong pull, and a pull altogether. Lift your hearts and voices in praise to God. Remember that we are now worshiping God."

Captain Kerr, who had a good voice, and was familiar with the favorite tunes in which the "Psalms of David" are sung in Scotland, struck up "Old Hundred." One by one they began to fall in ; and, as line after line was parceled out, they joined more and more heartily, until the good old tune came free and full from hundreds of lips, and the whole island, bay, and farther shore echoed with these closing words of the excellent Doddridge :

"Such blessings from thy gracious hand,
Our humble prayers implore,

And thou shall be our chosen God,
And portion evermore."

"Now, men," said the preacher, "you have sung nobly, and, blessed be God! you are behaving yourselves well. I am happy to see it. Let us now look up to God in prayer." He closed his eyes, clasped his hands, and gave free course to a full heart in a fervent address to the Almighty.

At the close of the prayer, he saw that the tears had been streaming down the cheeks of many of his hard-visaged hearers. Taking fresh courage from this manifest blessing of God, he then read, in the most impressive manner of which he was capable, the fourth and fifth chapters of the second epistle to the Corinthians. They gave a good degree of attention as he proceeded. "Now, lads!" he added, "you are behaving well, and I am glad to see that you have so much respect for the worship of God. You sung very well the first time; come, let us sing another hymn from the little book." Once more they made the island ring with the good old church-music, endeared by a thousand recollections of the far-off land, and their native cot.

The missionary began now to seat his audience. "Come, my good lads!" he said, "don't stand up here any longer; gather round me here, and sit down on the rocks, and make yourselves comfortable, while I endeavor to preach to you the good word of the Lord." The congregation were presently seated, with the exception of a gang of five or six scores of vicious-looking characters, who appeared to be at the beck and call of two or three blackguards, on the right of the mass of the audience, and at some little distance. He soon observed that they seemed to be planning to break up the meeting by a tumultuous rush upon the missionary. Holding up his finger, and then pointing at them, he said, "Come, come, you fellows there, I see what you are about; and now, if you do n't stop your mischief, and break up all your contrivances, my good friends around me here will soon put you straight. So, the sooner you break up, the better. Come and take your seats here along with your other companions, and I will tell you things that will do your souls good." They complied with the invitation, and presently were all seated in expectation of the sermon.

In proceeding to preach, he called their attention to the first clause of the eleventh verse of the fifth chapter of the second epistle to the Corinthians: "Knowing, therefore, the terror of the Lord, we persuade men." He began the discourse with an exhibition of some of the threatenings, or terrors, of the Lord, addressed to the ungodly; and showed how surely those threatenings would be executed against all who died in unbelief and impenitence. He then showed them who the ungodly were, and spoke of them under several classes; such as drunkards, liars, swearers, sabbath-breakers, profane persons, idlers, and evil-doers. The evils of drunkenness were spread before them in the first place, as one of the sins against which the wrath of God has been revealed. They were reminded of them by an appeal to their own experience, and especially to the consequences of their recent course of conduct, as well as by what they had seen and known of these evils in the lives and deaths of their comrades and others. Earnest expostulations were used with them against any further indulgence in this worse than brutal vice.

Mr. Bertram also presented before them the iniquity of malice, hatred, revenge, and all strife and contention; he endeavored to make them ashamed of their violence one toward another; to show them that their hands were not made to beat and tear one another's flesh, but to minister to their comfort, and the good of their fellow-creatures. He told them that "God is love," and that the kindness of the Almighty, as well as His holy word, taught us to love one another, and give up the practice of fighting with our fellow-men.

The sin and evil of swearing were next dwelt upon, and they were told how exceedingly provoking it was to God, as well as how profitless and unreasonable it was. As he drew near the close, he said, " And, now, let me persuade you, men, after I have left the island this morning, and you no longer hear my voice among you, to sit down together in groups about the island, and read to each other these beautiful religious tracts that I have brought down with me from the Cape of Good Hope. Some of you, I know, can read, if others cannot; and, as you have been helping one another in the dreadful work of destroying your bodies, breaking God's laws, and ruining your souls, do try and help one another, through the reading of these tracts, to repent of your wickedness, return to God, and lead new lives. Let me also add, if you are permitted to live until to-morrow morning, just go about your work like good fellows. God never intended us to be idle:

> 'And Satan finds some mischief still
> For idle hands to do.'

Let me persuade you to go right about it on Monday morning, and labor honestly and industriously in your calling, as God and man would have you do, for your daily bread. And now let me say, in conclusion, if you will be persuaded to take this kind advice, I will come back again, and preach to you, if the Lord spares my life, next Sabbath morning. What say you, men, shall I come?"

With one voice almost they cried out, " Come,

sir! Oh! come. We like your preaching, sir, and will be glad to have you come again; and then we will have a far better place prepared for you." "Blessed be God!" he responded; "it is not guns and pistols that you want; it is not cutlasses, and ships-of-war, and cannon-balls that will serve to subdue you. No: it is the blessed gospel of Christ; it is the precious blood of Jesus; it is the Spirit of God. Now, men, you have behaved well, very well; blessed be God! You sung well at the commencement of the service, but you will sing better at the conclusion."

Another hymn was given out, that was sung with a right good-will, and the meeting was closed with prayer and the benediction. He then took leave of them, invoking upon them, as they heartily responded to his parting salutations, the blessing of the Almighty; and, accompanied by his two friends, he stepped into the boat at the end of the jetty, and soon made his way down the harbor to the principal anchorage. But, not as they came, went they back. Captains Mosey and Kerr, who kept their peace before, were now full of what they had seen and heard. They declared that the humble missionary of the Cross, with the simple gospel of Christ, had accomplished far more that morning than her Majesty's ship-of-war, with all her carnal weapons. Mr. Bertram preached in the P.M. to the shipmasters and the crews on board, and with none the less force from the remarkable experience of the morning. Thus ended his second Sabbath in Saldanha Bay.

The developments of the following morning were awaited with no little interest at the anchorage. Very soon after the rising of the sun, it became apparent that the mutineers had returned to duty. The luggage-boats were put in requisition, and the most active operations of business were resumed. "The sword of the Lord and of Gideon" had triumphed. The walls of opposition had fallen down at the blowing of the Gospel trumpet. The weapons of a spiritual warfare, more potent than bristling bayonets, had proved "mighty, through God, to the pulling down of strongholds." The island presented an appearance of busy and orderly industry, as opposite as possible to the scenes of the preceding fortnight. The quarreling, fighting, and horrid dissipation of those two weeks had given place to peace, contentment, diligence, promptness, and sobriety. Let God be praised, and man adore!

It was no fitful movement. Throughout the week, the bay and island presented the same busy and happy scenes. The following Sabbath morning brought with it a perfect readiness on the part of the shipmasters to send Mr. Bertram to the island. On his arrival he was greeted with a hearty welcome by his grateful congregation, whose appearance presented a striking contrast to the tumultuous and riotous assembly into which he had cast himself, a week before, unheralded and unbidden. The bloody faces had been washed; the soiled and torn garments had been exchanged for clean and tidy clothes; and a much more convenient place had been prepared for the field-preacher, whose ministrations they now received with the utmost gladness.

Thus, for several weeks, the humble missionary of the Cross, who, by God's grace, had achieved a nobler triumph than any ever won on battle-fields in "garments rolled in blood," continued to preach to the temporary inhabitants of Malagas Island, every Sabbath morning, with increasingly happy results; and in the afternoon to the shipmasters at the anchorage within the bay. Every facility for the prosecution of his voluntary mission was afforded by the masters of vessels; and, to their credit it should be spoken, they gave heed themselves to the word preached. Grateful for what they had seen and heard, they appeared to be impressed also with a vivid sense of the obligations of religion, and to feel a sincere desire, some of them, at least, for a personal interest in the grace of the Gospel. This they manifested, not only by a most respectful attendance on the Sabbath services, but by coming together for religious services occasionally during the week, on board several of the vessels, where such meetings were held. Death was not idle during this period, as he never is; and several of the shipmasters as well as seamen, by some casualty, or virulent disorder, were summoned to their audit with the Great Judge. They slept the sleep that knows no waking until the last great morning dawns. It was customary when a seaman was taken sick to send for Mr. Bertram to read, and talk, and pray with him, almost as regularly as to send for the physician; and at the death of any of them he performed the solemn services of prayer and exhortation, so appropriate to the last sad scene of our mortal pilgrimage.

While thus diligently and usefully employed, Mr. Bertram received a communication from Cape Town, conveying the distressing intelligence, that his only daughter, a lovely child, six years old, had been run over in the street near his dwelling-place, by an eight-horse wagon, and was lying in a very critical state, having barely escaped with life. His immediate return to the Cape was required, and the unwelcome information soon flew from ship to ship. The deepest sympathy was universally expressed for their beloved chaplain, in his affliction, and regret at the necessity of their being deprived of his inestimable services. A polite and affectionate note was sent him, requesting him to deliver a farewell discourse the same evening on board of Captain Kerr's ship.

In the evening about sixty or seventy shipmasters assembled in the "Fama," to whom he preached as requested. At the conclusion of the service, three of the shipmasters rose, and, approaching the preacher, stated, that they had been appointed by the masters of vessels in the harbor, to present him, in their name, with a purse of gold, which they put into his hands, with their most grateful thanks for his kind services, and for what God had enabled him to do for them by the preaching of His blessed gospel; and that they further desired him to purchase, from the contents of the purse, a silver cup, as a memorial of their gratitude, and to place upon it this inscription:—

"Purchased by request out of a purse of gold presented to the Rev. James M'Gregor Bertram by about fifty commanders of vessels and other gentlemen at Saldanha Bay, as a mark of esteem for his zeal, manifested for the moral and spiritual improvement of their crews and workmen employed on Malagas Island, in preaching among them the unsearchable riches of Christ.

DEPUTATION,

CAPTAIN ENGLISH, CAPTAIN NEIL,

CAPTAIN AYMERS.

Saldanha Bay, 10th June, 1845.

Mr. Bertram expressed his deep sense of their

kindness, and assured them that, when he came down from the Cape to preach among them, he had no expectation of receiving a shilling for his services ; that he came not for their silver or gold, but purely for the salvation of their souls; and that in receiving the purse he had to request them, that, instead of a cup, they would allow him to purchase a silver watch, of which he stood in need, and to have the inscription placed upon its case. It was a very tender and affecting scene. They parted, to meet no more, in many cases, until they should meet "at the judgment-seat of Christ."

On the following day he took his departure by land, and at the expiration of four days, being assisted by the Dutch farmers in passing from one settlement to another, he arrived at Cape Town, and had the happiness to find that his daughter, (under the kind and unremitting attentions of Dr. Abercrombie, to whom he will ever feel under the deepest obligations,) was rapidly, by the blessing of God, recovering from her injuries. His journey gave him also an admirable opportunity to see something of the beautiful scenery and exuberant fertility of Southern Africa. The watch was purchased, and, with the inscription prepared at Saldanha Bay, has become his inseparable companion.

At the time of Col. Napier's visit to the Bay, about the first of October, 1846, nearly sixteen months after Mr. Bertram's sojourn of eight or ten weeks, "a solitary bark lay motionless at anchor in one of the small rocky inlets of the gulf; the guano had disappeared, and the penguins had resumed their sway over the gray rocks of Malagas Island; "a scaffolding or two, on the water's edge, to facilitate the embarkation of the manure, were the only remaining indications of the busy scenes which had of late enlivened its now abandoned shores." The revenue accruing to the government, at the rate of twenty shillings per ton, is said to have reached the sum of £200,000, leaving a vast sum to swell the fortunes of the principal dealers in this lucrative traffic.

Thus helpful is the gospel to the pursuits of commerce, and to the productiveness of human labor. The merchants of Great Britain and America might well afford to plant a seaman's chaplain in every sea-port on the globe. They would be vastly the gainers by such an operation. Remember, ye merchant princes! the hardy sons of the ocean, by whom ye have your wealth. Think of them, care for them, save them from perdition. The least that you can do for them is, to give them the gospel. You cannot give them a greater gift. Withhold not that.

CHAPTER IV.

LIFE AT ST. HELENA.

"A MAN'S heart deviseth his way; but the Lord directeth his steps." The hand of God is very often distinctly seen in the shaping of human counsels, as it may always eventually be seen in human history. In cases not a few, enterprises of immense importance have been undertaken, not as the result of far-seeing calculation on the part of the agents enlisted in the work, but in obedience to some unforeseen and unthought-of movement in the operations of Divine Providence. The very failure of our own plans, the disappointments to which we are subjected, and the prevalence of opposite counsels, serve frequently to bring us into spheres of labor, and positions of influence, where we can accomplish far more, for God and man, than if our fondest hopes, and wisest counsels, had been fulfilled.

"Our indiscretion sometimes serves us well,
When our deep plots do pall; and that should teach us,
There 's a divinity that shapes our ends,
Rough-hew them how we will."

Previous to the return of Mr. Bertram from Saldanha Bay, the good hand of the Lord was preparing for him, without his knowledge, and without so much as a thought of any such thing, a field of labor, and a home, in the midst of the vast Atlantic. One of the inhabitants of Cape Town, a young man, who had resided there about five years, and had recently been converted to God through the labors of some of the missionary brethren at the Cape, resolved to make a visit to the island of St. Helena, the place of his nativity. To this he was actuated in part, by a natural desire, not only to see again his friends and kindred, but to tell them also what the Lord had done for his soul. When he looked around on the spiritual desolation of his kinsmen, and their fellow-islanders; when he saw that thousands of immortal beings were living at St. Helena, in almost entire disregard, and many of them in ignorance, of the "Great Salvation," his heart was stirred within him, and he longed to do something for their spiritual good.

On the return of this young man to the Cape, he could not but tell, to his Christian friends, what he had seen and heard, of the destitution in his native isle. So deplorable was the picture that he presented, and so earnest was he in his representations, as greatly to move the hearts of the ministers and their people. They took counsel together, and in the name of the Lord resolved to undertake the enterprise of sending a missionary to St. Helena.

It was while the Spirit of God was thus directing their minds to this new field of labor, that Mr. Bertram unexpectedly returned from his successful mission at Saldanha Bay. Immediately on his return, he received a visit from his friend and brother, the Rev. George Morgan ; who was accompanied by the Hon. Judge Williams, who had come thither from India for the recovery of his health ; a man of the greatest devotion, and of most exemplary life, as a follower of Christ. They came to press upon his consideration the mission to St. Helena. They urged him to abandon his original intention of penetrating into the interior of the continent, and called his attention to the fact, that here was as wide a sphere of influence opened before him as he could expect or wish. They represented that a large number of the population of the island were in an exceedingly benighted state, and expressed their astonishment, that no Protestant dissenting missionaries had been sent thither from Great Britain or America, while, it was confidently stated, the Church of Rome were contemplating the establishment of a mission among the natives of the island. They entreated him to go and take possession of the ground, before the arrival of the two priests and emissaries of the Pope.

As the proposition was entirely unlooked-for, and the sphere of service novel, Mr. Bertram, like a prudent man, desired time to inform himself, and, as in duty bound, ask counsel of God. In all former emergencies of the kind, he had betaken himself to the throne of grace, with the prayer of the converted Saul, and asked, "Lord! what wilt thou have me to do?" and never in vain. A voice from the inner sanctuary had again and again responded, "This is the way, walk ye in it." Some of his good brethren at the Cape would have had him remain there, believing that he was more needed in that port than even at St. Helena. But what was to become of the good work so happily commenced at Saldanha Bay? His return to that station was urgently entreated. A letter had been addressed to the Rev. George Morgan, begging him to use his influence to send Mr. Bertram back again to Malagas Island.

"I have taken the liberty," says Mr. Johnstone, June 23d, 1845, "of addressing you these few lines, at the request of the seamen and European laborers employed on this island; and they much regret that the Rev. Mr. Bertram's stay was not of a longer duration, as his visits to this island proved a most beneficial service to the poor islanders; and every Sunday morning a general inquiry takes place, to know if his visits will be renewed, as he would be hailed with enthusiasm, and a most welcome return." Mr. Tait also wrote to Rev. J. C. Brown, by the same conveyance, and said, "It would be doing an act of charity, by those who can order the same, to let us have our much and late respected friend again with us for a short period, as his services would be hailed with the greatest esteem."

At the expiration of about ten or twelve days, the path of duty became so plain, that he determined to make a visit, at least, to St. Helena, preparatory to the commencement of a mission in that island, should the way be clear. Measures were immediately taken, on the part of the Rev. Messrs. Morgan, Brown, Hodgson, Beck, and Ridsdale, with other Christian friends, to provide an outfit for the missionary. The following statement was drawn up as the basis of an appeal for contributions to the enterprise:

"The Island of St. Helena, though hitherto unoccupied by any missionary society, presents a most interesting field for missionary labor. The population of the island amounts to between five and six thousand, of whom about two thirds are people of color. A large proportion of this latter class is scattered over the island, and left too destitute of religious instruction; while many who are within reach of the means of grace are living in a state of irreligion and immorality, and need the labors of a zealous missionary to stir them up to a due concern for the salvation of their souls. In addition to this all-important consideration, the 'signs of the times' render it extremely desirable that a Protestant missionary should enter on this promising field of labor without delay. Nor is it unworthy of the true Christian philanthropist to regard, with peculiar interest, the spot where *Napoleon* terminated his career in exile and in death, and to cherish the fond desire, that *St. Helena* should obtain a far more glorious celebrity from the triumphs of the *Cross*.

"The Rev. J. M'Gregor Bertram, who has lately been laboring at Saldanha Bay, has expressed his willingness to proceed immediately to St. Helena, to preach the gospel to the destitute portion of its population; and it is proposed to raise a subscription to aid in defraying his expenses.

"It will be understood that those, who may be pleased to subscribe their names, do not in the least degree pledge themselves to repeat their contributions, the object being simply to enable Mr. Bertram to enter upon his benevolent enterprise without pecuniary embarrassment, leaving it to be determined by the result of his labors, whether he shall take up his permanent residence at St. Helena, or proceed to some other part of the world, whither Divine Providence may direct his steps."

To this paper were subscribed the following names, with the amount of their contributions:

Rev. George Morgan, Scottish Church.	Mr. W. Cairncross, Junior.
" J. C. Brown, Union Ch.	" T. Cairncross.
" T. L. Hodgson, Sup'dt. of Wesleyan Missions.	" Broadway.
" J. H. Beck, S'th African Missionary Society.	" J. Reid.
" B. Ridsdale, Wes. Miss.	" A. Hutchinson.
Mr. Alexander, B. C. S.	" C. S. Pillars.
" Hawkins, do.	" G. Thompson.
" Brown, do.	" Borrodailes.
" Williams, do.	" J. Lawton.
" W. Cairncross, Senior.	Dr. Abercrombie.
	Mr. Rutherford.
	" Solomon.
	A Friend, etc., etc., etc.

A similar statement also appeared, June 21st, in the "Commercial Advertiser," of Cape Town; and in the July number of "the Cape of Good Hope Christian Magazine," a monthly periodical of decided ability, which had been commenced in the preceding January. In answer to these appeals, a sum exceeding sixty-five pounds was contributed by the gentlemen above-named, of which nearly forty pounds were collected by the truly excellent Judge Williams, who had manifested so great an interest in the enterprise. Captain James Adams, of the brig "Velox," since deceased, very generously made him the offer of a free passage to the island; for which, and his subsequent kindness to one of Christ's disciples, he has ere this received, we doubt not, the reward promised by the Great Head of the Church to him who giveth a cup of water to any of His servants in the name of Christ. On Saturday, June 28th, Mr. Bertram bade farewell to his family, and, provided with letters to a worthy resident of the island, he set sail, with a favoring wind, for his future home.

St. Helena is a singular elevation of rock in the midst of the Atlantic Ocean, eighteen hundred miles from the Cape of Good Hope, twelve hundred miles from the nearest coast of Africa, two thousand miles from South America, and six hundred miles from the Island of Ascension, which is the nearest land. It lies in 15° 15′ south latitude, and 5° 49′ west longitude from Greenwich. Its extreme length is ten and a half miles; its breadth, six and three-quarter miles; and its circumference, twenty-eight miles. It contains an area of thirty thousand three hundred acres.

The island was discovered, May 21, 1502, by the Portuguese navigator, Juan de Nova Castella, and received its name in honor of the day of its discovery, the festival of "Saint Helena." Not a human being, probably, had ever before trodden its soil. An unbroken forest covered the island. Its shores abounded with seals, sea-lions, and wild-fowl. So it remained until the year

1513. Fernandez Lopez, a Portuguese nobleman, on his way home from India, where he had been mutilated for crime, by order of Governor Albuquerque, prevailed upon the captain to set him ashore on this uninhabited island, whose solitudes he preferred to the shame and contempt that awaited him in his native land. His situation having been made known to his friends in Portugal, they quickly furnished him with supplies of useful plants and trees, and various kinds of domestic animals, all which flourished and multiplied greatly. Lopez was suffered to remain only about four years, when the island was again left without a human tenant.

A somewhat different account is given by others; who say, that Governor Albuquerque, after the battle of Goa, condemned several of his countrymen, who had previously deserted, and who now fell into his power, to lose their noses, ears, right hands, and thumbs of their left hands, and to be sent in this condition to Portugal; but that they were all put on shore, with a few negroes, at St. Helena, with poultry of various kinds to serve for their subsistence.

The former authorities represent that it next became the abode of four negroes, who had escaped from a slave ship, and who shortly increased to twenty. The Portuguese, however, who had found the island a convenient place for obtaining a supply of fresh provisions, and feared lest the live-stock and fruits, which had vastly multiplied since the days of Lopez, would be entirely exhausted by the negroes, hunted them out and destroyed them. A Franciscan friar is said after this to have occupied the island alone for the space of fourteen years, until his death or removal by the Portuguese.

About the middle of the sixteenth century, the island appears to have been made a regular settlement, and to have been subjected to cultivation. It was visited, in June, 1588, by Sir Thomas Cavendish, on his return from a voyage around the world. A church had been erected, which he particularly describes. He speaks of the valley where it was built as extremely pleasant, and full of plants and fruit-trees, having long rows of lemon, citron, pomegranate, date, and fig-trees, nicely trimmed, and forming beautiful shady walks. He found great store of partridges, pheasants, turkeys, goats, and swine.

From this time it became a convenient stopping-place for English, Dutch, Spanish, and Portuguese vessels. It would sometimes be the case, that hostile vessels would meet here; and consequently naval battles be fought in the harbor, followed by the wanton destruction of the town and plantations, when the victors were at war with the Portuguese. On these accounts, the settlement was abandoned in the early part of the seventeenth century, and once more became desolate.

Several Portuguese sailors, having escaped from the wrecks of their two vessels, landed here in 1643, and again stocked the island with cattle, goats, swine, poultry, etc. Two years after, it came into the possession of the Dutch, who planted here a colony, but abandoned the island, when, in 1652, they formed their settlement at Table Bay. It came into the possession of the British government, under the Protectorate of Oliver Cromwell, shortly after, on occasion of a visit from the homeward-bound East India fleet. A fort was erected in 1658, by Captain Dutton, the first British governor, which was, after the Restoration, called "Fort James," in compliment to the Duke of York, from whom, also, the principal settlement at the anchorage received the name of "James' Town." Settlers were encouraged, and slaves were imported from Madagascar. Charles II. gave it by charter to the East India Company. It was visited by Rennefort in 1666, who found a population of about seventy whites, of whom twenty were females, besides a few negroes. The great fire of London in the same year added several colonists, who were driven abroad to amend their ruined fortunes.

It fell into the hands of the Dutch in 1672, but was recaptured in the following year by a squadron of British vessels under the command of Captain Munden; who succeeded by false colors in decoying and capturing six East Indiamen, and an outward-bound ship of the enemy; for which exploits he received the reward of knighthood. His name was also given to the point and fort on the left of the entrance to the harbor. In 1676, '7, and '8, the island became the abode of the youthful astronomer, Edmund Halley, who, at the age of twenty-two, visited the island to observe the transit of Venus; and, during his abode, made his observations of the fixed stars in the southern hemisphere, and formed them into constellations, of which he published an account in the following year. The hill on which his instruments were erected has since been known as "Halley's Mount," and has an elevation of two thousand four hundred and sixty-seven feet above the sea.

When the island was visited in 1691 by Captain Dampier, he found there a fort, with a garrison, "and a good number of great guns." The town was small, "the inhabitants having their plantations deeper into the country, which furnish them with potatoes, plantains, bananas, hogs, bullocks, cocks and hens, ducks, geese, and turkeys, in vast plenty." The latter years of the seventeenth century were characterized by frequent and violent disturbances at the island on account of taxes; which continued, more or less, until, in 1700, all the " spirit-stills" that had occasioned the trouble, were suppressed. During the following century the population continued to increase, and the products of the island were greatly multiplied. It prospered much at the close of the century under Governor Brooke, in whose time it was made a depot for training recruits for the armies of the East India Company, to the number of more than twelve thousand soldiers, and the fortifications were greatly strengthened. About two hundred Chinese laborers were introduced, in and shortly after 1810, as well as new colonists from England; so that a larger amount of land was speedily brought under cultivation.

The subsequent history of St. Helena is better known. On the 15th of October, 1815, a British squadron, under the command of Admiral Sir George Cockburn, cast anchor in James' Town Harbor, St. Helena. From the deck of the " Northumberland" ship-of-war, NAPOLEON BUONAPARTE gazed, with glass in hand, on his sepulchre. The next day beheld him treading that soil which he was never to leave with life. This island had been chosen as his place of confinement, because of its immense distance from every other inhabited coast, its complete isolation in the wide waste of waters, the perfect ease with which its walls of precipitous rock might be made impregnable, and the greater freedom that could be given to the imperial prisoner within his sea-girt fortress.

The government of the island, which to this period had been in the hands of the East India Company, was now surrendered to the crown. The military force was largely increased, and every accessible portion of the rocky coast put in a state of complete defense. Four or five hundred cannon, some of them thirty-two pounders, were mounted on the rocks and hills that commanded the harbor and avenues, so that the whole island bristled with munitions of war. The average annual charges were increased from £90,000 to £242,000 for seven years. The imprisonment of the Corsican, therefore, cost the British government not less than one million pounds sterling; from which they were relieved by the decease of their illustrious captive, May 6th, 1821. During the following year, the royal forces were removed, and the custody of the island reverted once more to the East India Company, in whose hands it remained until the year 1833, when, the Company having failed to secure a renewal of their ancient charter, it was finally relinquished to the crown of Great Britain. Since that time it has been put on the footing of a British colony, under the administration of a governor and council. It is garrisoned with a battalion of riflemen, and a detachment of artillery. The fortifications are forty-three, defended by two hundred and forty-three mortars, howitzers, and guns.

The brig Velox, with the first Protestant dissenting missionary that had ever sailed for St. Helena, to live and labor among its neglected population, arrived in James' Valley Bay, early on Monday, July 14th, 1845. The island may be seen at the distance of about forty miles, and then seems like a dense cloud, of an undulating outline, just within the horizon. The night prevented Mr. Bertram from obtaining a nearer view, until the brig had come close up to the rocky coast, which now frowned in gloomy grandeur almost overhead. A dark pile of rocks it seemed, rising precipitously out of the sea, roughly jagged at the sides, and peaked at the top, bare of verdure, with the exception of a small patch of moss here and there ; the vast mass looking like the summit of some lofty volcano, whose base is planted deep in the ocean, and rises from five hundred to twenty-seven hundred feet above the level of the sea. It forms a girdle of inaccessible precipices of basaltic rocks, some of them rent to their bases, and presenting immense and frightful chasms of the most fantastic shapes that can be thought of.

As the brig glided around the northeast corner of the island, in the usual track of vessels from "the Cape," point after point of the same grand and gloomy character was passed, until they came in sight of a small fort at the top of a rock, rising about five hundred feet from the sea, so abruptly, that a ship may pass in full sail within a few yards of its base. On rounding Munden's Point, below the fort just named, the striking panorama of James' Valley, on the northwest side of the island, came full in view. Directly in front of them, on the right of the anchorage, rose a lofty precipice, known as "Ladder Hill," surmounted, at an elevation of about eight hundred feet, by fortifications, and ascended by a circuitous road, cut with immense labor out of the face of the rock, for the convenience of carriages. The hill derives its name from an inclined railway, or ladder, extending almost directly from the fort down to the landing-place, for the conveyance of provisions and other supplies to the summit; which may also be ascended by pedestrians, although few can endure the fatigue. Over against this hill, another rocky ridge arose on the east, almost as high, called "Rupert's Hill." Between these two mountainous cliffs, a deep gorge was seen to extend, as through a natural gateway, into the interior; along which, and particularly at its lower termination, appeared a pretty cluster of white houses, embosomed in verdure, known as "James' Town," among which are seen most conspicuously the governor's house and an Episcopal church.

Almost as soon as the anchor was dropped,

Mr. James Morris—a resident of the town, to whom Mr. Bertram had been commended, in a letter of introduction from the Rev. T. L. Hodgson, Superintendent of the Wesleyan Missions in the Cape Colony, and who had learned by another arrival two days before that a missionary was coming—hastened on board, and, finding him, said, after reading Mr. Hodgson's letters—"Have you come here, Mr. Bertram, to preach Christ's Gospel?" "I have, by the will of God," was the prompt reply. "Do you intend to make the island your home?" "I do." "And pray, sir, who sent you here?" "Why, sir, I believe that God sent me here." "Well, my dear friend," said Mr. Morris, "there are only four or five persons on the island who know any thing about a work of grace in their hearts, and they have met twice a week for the last six months, to beseech God to send them a missionary to break to them the bread of life; and is it possible, that God has already heard our poor prayers, and sent you to minister to us in the name of the Lord? My dear sir, I cannot tell you how welcome you are."

Mr. Morris at once bade him accompany him to the shore, and take up his abode with him until he could be better accommodated; and his invitation was promptly accepted. Both persons and goods are landed at a jetty, the only one in the harbor, which is provided with cranes and stairs for the purpose, not very well adapted, however, for the accommodation of either. From the landing-place, a narrow road, lined with evergreen trees, of the banian species, called in Bengal, the peepul tree, leads along the face of the perpendicular cliff, toward the gate of the fortress and town, at the mouth of the valley or gorge, which is here crossed by a strong and lofty wall, pierced with embrasures, and mounted with guns. Before reaching the gate, a wide moat is crossed by a drawbridge. Beyond the gate the town resembles an orderly garrison; every portion of the gully over which it is built, and which, narrowing rapidly as it ascends, is nowhere more than six hundred yards wide, has been improved as much as possible. The houses are built along three principal streets, are generally of cut stone, and slated; but are seldom more than two stories in height. The gateway forms one side of the parade-ground, which is about two hundred feet square, and is kept very neatly. In two of the streets are found numerous shops, in which are to be had the produce of both hemispheres and continents. The principal street is Macadamized in the center, with pebble-walks on the sides, and extends the distance of a mile, with rows of the peepul tree, the most of the way, on either side. The scenery is altogether unique. The bold crags towering on either hand; the hills far away up the winding road that leads into the interior; and the broad expanse of ocean, the wide waste of waters in front, form one of the most picturesque scenes on which the eye can rest.

The house is shown in the town where Napoleon rested the first night after his landing. It is said to be the same that was occupied by the Duke of Wellington, when, on his way to India, he passed some weeks on the island. Singularly enough, Wellington was, at the time of Buonaparte's arrival, in the occupation of one of the ex-emperor's palaces. It is also said, to have been owing to a suggestion of the duke's, that St. Helena was chosen as the prison of Napoleon, the quick eye of the experienced soldier having discerned how admirably fortified it was by nature, and could be by art.

The coming of Mr. Bertram was soon made known to the little band of praying disciples at James' Town, who presently found him at the house of Mr. Morris, and with tears of joy made him welcome to St. Helena. Among them was an old soldier, who had spent his early life in the service of the East India Company, had for many years been put on the retired list, and was now living on a pension. Captain D. O'Connor was a godly man, of the Congregational denomination, who, for thirty years or more, had testified for God, like Lot in Sodom. His name and character were known throughout the tropics. He corresponded with good men abroad, and, among others, with the Rev. Rufus Anderson, D.D., of Boston, one of the Secretaries of the A. B. C. of Foreign Missions, from whom he used to receive, with the Annual Report of the American Board, a package of religious tracts, which he and his good lady took pleasure in distributing among the Europeans on the island. This valiant old soldier of the Cross, like blessed Simeon of old, was waiting for the consolation of Israel. He had attained a good age, and, like the ancient patriarch, "worshiped, leaning upon the top of his staff."

It was a joyful day to Captain O'Connor, when with his own eyes he beheld the missionary of the Cross, who had come to gather in Christ's scattered sheep, and to make St. Helena his home. Doubtless he said in his heart—"Lord! now lettest thou thy servant depart in peace, for mine eyes have seen thy salvation." Grasping Mr. Bertram by the hand, and with moistened eyes, he said—"I have long been praying, my dear sir, that some missionary of the Cross might be sent to preach to this perishing population. And now the day begins to dawn!" During the remaining twelve or fifteen months of his life, he continued the devoted friend of the missionary, and died, blessing God for all the good that he had lived to see accomplished.

Preparations were made for a sermon on the evening of the next day, Tuesday, at the house of Mr. Morris. The large dining-room, where the praying band had been wont to meet, was seated so as to hold about sixty persons, and was filled with an intelligent congregation of whites, to whom Mr. Bertram preached from Acts xvi., 14, 15: "And a certain woman, named Lydia, a seller of purple, of the city of Thyatira, which worshiped God, heard us; whose heart the Lord opened, that she attended unto the things which were spoken of Paul. And when she was baptized, and her household, she besought us, saying, If ye have judged me to be faithful to the Lord, come into my house, and abide there. And she constrained us." It was a word in season, and highly appropriate to the occasion.

He told them that the natural heart, universally, is closed against its Maker and Lord; that God had a key by which to open the heart, a wonder-working key; the plan, the shape, the design of which were devised in the counsels of heaven from eternity, and finished on earth, in Gethsemane and Calvary, when the Saviour of mankind travailed in the greatness of His strength, and gave birth to the world's redemption; that God had already opened millions of hearts with this key, and could as many more; and that he had brought that key—"the glorious gospel of the blessed God"—with him from the Cape of Good Hope, in the hope that He, who had there-with opened the heart of Lydia, would open the hearts also of many of the St. Helenians.

It was evident, from the number attending this first service, and the interest manifested by the audience, that a larger room would be needed. It pleased God to put it into the heart of an excellent lady, Mrs. Janisch, to open her parlor for the use of the missionary. She was the widow of the late Dutch consul, from whom she had been separated about twenty months. Her house was one of the largest in town, and she herself of the first respectability. Mr. Bertram very gratefully waited upon her, and arranged for a service there on Friday evening. Information of the appointment having been generally circulated, the place, large as it was, would not hold the people who came together to hear the word of God. It was a style of preaching to which they had never listened on that island. The chaplains, who alone had officiated there, were of the Church of England, and their preaching destitute of power and life, if not of godliness. When the people, therefore, heard a minister of Christ, pouring forth a burning stream of gospel-truth upon his hearers, they were most deeply interested. The Spirit of God appeared to be at work at the very first service, stirring up the sinner to think, and feel, and pray.

The great respectability of Mrs. Janisch, at whose house Mr. Bertram was permitted to hold his religious services on the Sabbath, as well as at other times, operated very favorably upon his enterprise. In that portion of the world, and generally in the British colonies, a wide chasm separates the crown officers and their families, from the households of the mechanics and tradesmen. Not seldom they have no more dealings one with another, in matters of social intercourse, than had the Jews and Samaritans of old. The former pride themselves on their education, official position, and fortune. They are the aristocracy; far more consequential than the same class at the court of St. James, and more difficult of approach. When Mr. Bertram was introduced, by a minister of the gospel, in a book-store at Boston, to his Excellency, Governor Briggs, and saw nothing but a plain Yankee farmer, in appearance, dressed and demeaning himself like any other man, and neither exacting nor receiving any other testimonials of respect from his fellow-citizens than are paid to one another in the ordinary intercourse of well-bred gentlemen; and afterward, at Pittsfield, Massachusetts, was sought out by the governor, and invited to his hospitable mansion, where the door was opened by his son, and his reception was as frank and genial as if he had been an intimate friend of the family; he could scarcely believe his own senses; it was so entirely different from the cold, stately, ceremonious, and frequently pompous receptions of colonial governors, who seem to regard themselves as representatives of Imperial Majesty, and bound to keep themselves at a respectful distance from men of non-official dignity.

In justice, however, to a most worthy servant of the British crown, it should be said, that his Excellency, Lieutenant-Colonel HAMILTON TRELAWNY, the Governor of St. Helena, showed no little kindness to Mr. Bertram, and proved himself a gentleman in every sense of the word. During the trials to which the missionary was subjected subsequently, he threw around him the shield of his official protection, and, at his death, some two years after the commencement of the mission, Mr. Bertram mourned as for a father departed. Owing, in part at least, to the countenance given by the governor, whose daughter, with her husband, became an attendant on his ministry, he obtained a hearing from the most respectable families in the town.

Very shortly after he began to preach at the house of Mrs. Janisch, he learned from this worthy widow, that she was greatly distressed on account of her eldest son, Hudson, who, at his father's decease, had been left, next to his mother, in charge of the family. For some time he had proved a worthy helper to his widowed parent, but latterly had associated with giddy young men, was becoming addicted to late hours, and somewhat skeptical. She wished Mr. Bertram to embrace a favorable opportunity of counseling him in private. He had been absent in the interior, on a frolic, when his mother's house was first opened for preaching. On his return the next morning, he remonstrated with his mother, on the impropriety of making her parlor "a meeting-house," and somewhat angrily insisted on her withdrawing the permission that she had given. To this she could by no means give her assent; but said: "You must come yourself, my son, and hear the missionary, and if you should not be pleased, it will be a very easy matter for us to say, that it will no longer be convenient to open our house for preaching."

On the Sabbath, July 20th, Mr. Bertram preached at nine o'clock, A.M.; the hour having been appointed so as not to conflict with the service in the church at a quarter to eleven o'clock; and so deep was the impression, that almost the whole congregation were in tears. Mr. HUDSON R. JANISCH was present. At the close of the service, he met his mother in the drawing-room, and said: "Do not say any thing, mother, to Mr.

Bertram about not preaching here again. Those are solemn things we have heard this morning." He retired to his chamber, with the arrows of conviction rankling in his heart, and began to weep and pray. Not long after, he called at the house of Mr. Morris, (at whose dwelling Mr. Bertram was entertained as a most welcome guest, free of charge, for several weeks after his arrival,) made known to the missionary the distress of his soul, and was gladly instructed by him in the way of salvation. About five weeks from that time, he found "joy and peace in believing," at a prayer-meeting held at the house of the only American lady on the island.

The conversion of Mr. Janisch was soon noised abroad, and produced a deep sensation. He was universally regarded as not having his superior, for talents and education, among the young men of St. Helena. No expense had been spared, by his deceased father, in preparing him for public life. He occupied a place of distinguished trust in the employ of the government. The Home dispatches mostly passed through his hands, and, it was supposed, proceeded in some cases from his own pen. His appearance was also very prepossessing, being tall and of good proportions. Having found peace with God, he gave himself fully to the service of his Maker, and cast in his influence with that of Mr. Bertram, to whom he afterward became an invaluable helper. His noble mother, who moved in the highest circles of society, had hitherto been a stranger to experimental piety. But He, who opened the heart of Lydia, opened the eyes and heart of her who had opened her doors for His ambassador, and she too was soon found among the happy subjects of redeeming grace. Salvation literally came to her house, and several of her family were brought into the kingdom of Christ. Three daughters, also, of Captain Pritchard, one of whom has since become the wife of Mr. Janisch, were also brought to believe in Christ, and, with many others, in similar circles, to rejoice in hope of the glory of God. A blessed revival of religion had commenced, which resulted, within a few weeks, in the hopeful conversion of about fifty souls.

A few days after the arrival of Mr. Bertram, inquiry having been made as to the Missionary Society by whom he had been sent to the island, and the fact having been made known, that he came at his own charges, and received no salary from any source whatever, several individuals drew up and subscribed the following paper:

"James' Town, St. Helena, *July 23d*, 1845.

"Dear Sir:

"Having understood that it is your intention to request Mrs. Bertram and children (with the blessing of the Almighty), to join you upon the return of the brig 'Velox' to this island—We, the undersigned, your friends and sincere well-wishers, being desirous that your sojourn among us should be more permanent than it otherwise would be, if separated from your wife and family, beg, in furtherance of your intention, to present you with the amount affixed opposite our respective names, which we earnestly hope will meet with your acceptance.

"We beg to offer our sincere wishes for the health and happiness of yourself, Mrs. Bertram, and children, and that your residence among us may be mutually beneficial to yourself, and, dear sir,

"YOUR SINCERE FRIENDS AND WELL-WISHERS."

This very complimentary note, written only nine days after his arrival, was signed by Captain O'Connor, Messrs. S. & J. Scott, Mr. W. Carroll, U. S. Consul, Messrs. T. Charlett, J. Elliot, and H. R. Janisch, with Mrs. Galbraith and several others; and the sum presented was £20, or about one hundred dollars. Captain Adams, of the Velox, very generously offered a free passage to Mrs. Bertram and her two children, as he had to her husband; and about the middle of September, they embarked at Cape Town, on the Velox, for St. Helena, where they arrived about the first of October, and were welcomed by a host of ardent friends, whom God had raised up for the missionary and his family.

The house of Mrs. Janisch served to accommodate the increasing congregation for a short time only. The blessing of God had so manifestly rested on the undertaking from the very day of Mr. Bertram's landing, as to make it evident, that a permanent and more commodious place of worship must be procured. He was under the necessity of making the appeal—"The place is too strait for me; give place to me, that I may dwell." Application was made, but without success, for the use of one of the public schools. Better success attended the request for the use of a school-room, occupied by Mr. Thompson, the teacher of a private school; but this, which they could use only in the evening of other days than the Sabbath, also proved insufficient. Yet thronged as were the places of their assembling together, so much so that the people frequently crowded around the doors and windows, and stood in the open streets to hear the word of God, they were not able to furnish themselves with better accommodations for about ten weeks.

It was determined to call a meeting of the friends of the enterprise, on the 30th of July, only sixteen days after Mr. Bertram's arrival, to consult on the propriety of securing the erection or purchase of a mission house. Of this meeting, Mr. Janisch, who was appointed its secretary, gave the following account, two days after, in a letter to the Rev. George Morgan, of Cape Town:

"St. Helena, 1*st August*, 1845.

"Rev. Sir:

"It affords me much pleasure to inform you, that the views of yourself and worthy supporters, in sending the Rev. Mr. Bertram among us, have met with great success, and bid fair to be attended with a prosperity worthy of the cause. In furtherance of your intentions, a subscription has been set on foot for raising the means of building a mission house (or chapel), and on the first meeting for the purpose, £163 were subscribed, and, we have every reason to add, with a readiness and cheerfulness highly gratifying to every one truly interested in the good cause.

"It was also proposed, and carried by unanimous assent, that our most heartfelt and sincere thanks be conveyed to yourself and the other friends associated with you, who have so liberally furnished the means, under God, for the coming of our reverend friend among us.

"I doubt not you will be highly gratified to know, that our worthy governor's family attended a meeting held last evening; as their countenance of it must undoubtedly have great influence over the many, who are guided by example even more than precept, and will tend greatly to remove any unfounded prejudice which may exist.

"Trusting you will convey to your friends the united thanks which I have been requested to tender you, and with a confident hope of the continuance of their support, I have the honor to remain, etc."

At this meeting, Mr. Carroll proposed that a sum of £500 be raised, for the purpose of providing for the congregation a place of worship; and a committee, consisting of Captain O'Connor, Thomas Charlett, Esq., Messrs. William Carroll, Hudson R. Janisch, and five others, was appointed to ascertain what could be done for the accommodation of the worshipers. As their necessities were urgent, and they could not wait until a building could be erected for their use, they were authorized to procure the largest stone edifice in the town that could be purchased. A large stone dwelling-house in the central part of the town, directly opposite the officers' barracks, belonging to a lady in India, was purchased of her agent for £550, subject to the ratification of the owner. Possession was immediately given, on the condition of an annual rent, should the owner refuse them the privilege of purchase.

Measures were at once taken to alter, repair,

and furnish the building, for the two-fold purpose of a house of worship, and a dwelling-place for the missionary and his family. All this, however, could not be accomplished in less than about two months.

In the mean time, Mr. Bertram continued at his work.* After the novelty of the occasion had passed, and the evangelical style and matter of his preaching became more fully known, some of his early hearers began to be offended. "From that time many of his disciples went back, and walked no more with him." This defection of some of the families of the place arose from the opposition made to him by the ecclesiastical authorities of the town.

The colony was provided with two clergymen of the Church of England, in the pay of the government, with large salaries, one of whom was called the colonial, and the other, the military chaplain. The former ministered to the European residents, and the other to the soldiers. They were both of the Oxford School, and fully embraced the Romanizing doctrines of Dr. Pusey and the Tractarians. They were great sticklers for the dogmas of apostolical succession, consubstantiation, baptismal regeneration, and the *opus operatum* of the sacraments. They were,

* See Appendix, A

as a matter of course, greatly alarmed, when they heard that a dissenting preacher had come to take up his abode on the island; and still more so, when Sabbath after Sabbath, and night after night, they saw the people flocking to hear him. They endeavored to dissuade the community from giving him any countenance. But when they prevailed nothing, and it appeared as if the whole town would go after him, they proclaimed in private and in public, that "the Church was in danger." To this it was very properly replied, that if such was really the case, it could not be Christ's Church; for that never was, and never will be, in danger. Christ had promised that the gates of hell should never prevail against it.

Several of the Oxford Tracts were put into free circulation; particularly the Tract of Archdeacon Wilberforce, on "Disunion." The cry of "Schism!" was now raised, and the people were told, that it was a grievous sin against God and His Church, to attend upon the ministry of a man, on whose head the apostolical hands of some lord bishop had never been laid; that such a man, whatever he might pretend, and however he might find favor with men, could find no favor with God, was no minister of Christ, and nothing better than a wolf in sheep's clothing, a minister of Satan, an impostor. They warned the people, to stand aloof from him, lest they also should partake in the plagues which were sure, sooner or later, to come upon him and his adherents. They bade the people bring their children to them to be duly regenerated, made members of Christ's body, and inheritors of the kingdom of heaven, in the waters of holy baptism; and assured them, that if their children died without this ordinance, they could never be saved; and their bodies could be buried only in the shades of evening, or by night.

But none of these things moved him, against whom they were aimed, from his purpose of preaching the unsearchable riches of Christ. Controversy was avoided, and the truth plainly and pointedly preached. The work of grace ceased not, "and believers were the more added to the Lord."

The mission house was completed, and set apart for the worship of God, early in October. The services of dedication were graciously owned of God, and attended with the deepest interest by a crowded assembly. The following letter, written on the 8th of November to a friend at Cape Town, and published in the Cape Magazine for January, 1846, makes mention of this event, and gives other interesting particulars of the progress of the good work:

"Five weeks ago we entered into the new mission house, a very neat and comfortable place in every sense of the word. So much zeal and energy had been displayed by the *then* few friends of Mr. Bertram, to procure this place, and make it suitable as a place of worship, that, on the day it was opened, Mr. Bertram was quite overcome with joy that the Lord had thus prospered him, and provided a place where prayer should in future be made. All the service was beautifully appropriate. The afternoon's discourse was an exposition of the word 'Gospel;' and, I can assure you, the hearts of many appeared touched. The room is calculated to hold three hundred persons, and during the last three weeks many have not been able to find a seat. It is open *every* evening in the week, Mondays excepted, and a *Bethel* it is indeed. As the attendance increased, it was proposed that a certain sum should be raised for Mr. Bertram's support, and in less than a week £100 were subscribed; and it is supposed that the mission-box will yield about £50 more per annum! This you would call great doings, could you but witness the shameful opposition and party-spirit prevalent here. Many persons are convinced of sin, and some of influence are among those who are showing their faith by their works. The great interest in things spiritual felt by the soldiers is surprising. About twenty of them went to Mr. Bertram on Monday last, and asked permission to have an unfinished room in his yard as a place for prayer. Mr. Bertram immediately consented, and, during their hours for meals, they are engaged, heart and hand, in getting the room in order."

Another letter, written about two months later, and published in the Cape Magazine for March, 1846, after giving an account of the interesting exercises in the chapel on Christmas Day, and on New Year's Eve, which were very much thronged, and deeply solemn, adds the following:

"Mr. Bertram's ministry is assuredly crowned with success; and, I trust, he has, and will have, souls to his hire in this place. You would be pleased with our neat little chapel, and the commodious dwelling occupied by the minister; truly it seems peculiarly adapted in every respect, and to have come into the hands of the committee as of God's providing.

"Wonders have been done at St. Helena within the last few months, which, had any one foretold a year ago, he would have found skeptical hearers; yet I fear poor temporal support is to be found for Mr. Bertram on this barren spot. Of this he seems totally regardless, assured that the 'Lord will provide' as long as he is engaged in his Master's work. The *will* is not wanting, I firmly believe, among his hearers; but they are, almost all, of the poorest of the community. Should help be wanting, I do hope our neighbor Colony, who so kindly and nobly came forward to send the man of God to us, will not withhold further aid.

"A good work has commenced among the soldiers, to some of whom Mr. Bertram's ministry has been greatly blessed. The chapel is situated just opposite the lower end of the officers' parade, close to the barracks. An outer room of the building, to which there is access, without any interference with the dwelling, Mr. Bertram allows the soldiers exclusively for their own use; it is so close to their barracks, that they can hear the slightest bugle call, and is, consequently, peculiarly convenient to them. They repair there at any and all hours, when not on duty, for private or for social prayer. If they have but a few minutes to spare, they can thus turn it to the best account. They have stated meetings for religious exercises, also; two pious sergeants are among them. These two were at first the only soldiers that attended the chapel, but two or three at a time have become anxious about their eternal interests, and there are now more than a dozen altered characters among them, some of whom there is every reason to believe are savingly converted. The colored people also flock to hear, and Mr. Bertram's visits among the sick have been much blessed. What a blossoming in this moral wilderness! 'It is the Lord's doing, and wondrous in our eyes.'"

The good work of grace that was thus begun at James' Town, was not confined to that narrow valley. Other portions of the island were still more in need of the missionary's attentions. The population is considerably dispersed, and many of them quite remote from the seat of government. Their number is about seven thousand, of whom about two thousand are whites, or of European origin; of these, frôm five to seven hundred are attached to the army. Something like one thousand liberated Africans, brought in by the British cruisers from captured slave-ships, who have chosen to remain, by the consent of the governor, are employed as hired servants. Slavery, of course, does not exist. It was in the process of extinction before the passing of the British Emancipation Act, by which every slave in the British Empire obtained his freedom.

In addition, there are about four thousand natives. These are the descendants of the first settlers—Portuguese, East Indians, Africans, and British soldiers—who for several generations have been intermingled in almost every variety, and formed a race peculiar to the island, of a dark copper-color. These were all in a state of bondage formerly, and were left, after their emancipation, in the same miserable state of spiritual ignorance in which they and their fathers had been kept, generation after generation. In some cases the African blood predominates; but in other instances, and for the most part, they have long, glossy black hair, like the American Indians, and expressive features. These last are generally possessed of considerable intelligence and shrewdness, and are capable of a high degree of cultivation.

Not long after Mr. Bertram's arrival, and while he was breasting the waves of ecclesiastical opposition, he was waited upon by Captain MAPLETON, the principal magistrate of the island, who gave him a hearty welcome, and said, "I am glad to see you here on our island, Mr. Bertram, preaching the gospel of Christ. If any part of the world needs the gospel, we need it here. But you do not intend, I trust, to confine your labors to the town. Come over, sir, to Sandy Bay Valley, where I live, and where there is a great number of natives, who never in all their lives heard a gospel sermon in their valley. Come over, and preach to those poor neglected souls; and when you come, put up at my house. My lady will be glad to see you, and will make you as comfortable as possible. I am not a religious man myself; but I truly respect religion, and know that I ought to possess it. It would give me pleasure to see all our population put in possession of its blessings."

A call so earnest, from the honored lips of so

worthy a magistrate, was not to be slighted. Mr. Bertram conferred about it with Mr. Thomas Charlett, a respectable merchant in James' Town, and one of the first fruits of his ministry in St. Helena; and he said, "Yes, Mr. Bertram, go; it is just the very thing that should be done. Go, and I will go with you; I will order a couple of horses, and we 'll ride over to Sandy Bay, as Captain Mapleton desires. I know a respectable and worthy couple there, William Lambe and his wife, who live on the produce of a fine garden, about in the center of the valley, who will be very glad to see you. I think that they will let you have the use of a part of their new house in which to make a commencement."

It was the morning of a beautiful day in summer—December or January—when Messrs. Bertram and Charlett mounted their steeds, and set forth on their benevolent excursion across the island. In a few minutes they were climbing the steeps of Ladder Hill, on the right of the town and bay. No little nerve is required in passing over this precipitous road, that in most places is cut out of the side of the hill, and supported on the outer side by almost perpendicular walls. About half way up the hill, the zig-zag path is blasted out of the rocks, and is completely overhung by large masses of stone, which seem to be destitute of a sufficient prop, and threaten the passer-by with an instant crash, and hopeless destruction. This remarkable and fearful pass is called "Col. Pearce's Revenge."

At the summit of the hill, a sublime prospect presents itself to the visitor. The mighty ocean, stretching far away to the north and west, vast, boundless, fathomless, ever in motion, ever changing, and yet ever the same, lies at your feet:

> "Glorious mirror! where the Almighty's form
> Glasses itself in tempests; in all time,
> Calm or convulsed—in breeze, or gale, or storm,
> Dark-heaving; boundless, endless, and sublime,
> The image of eternity—the throne
> Of the Invisible."

The town, at the base of the hill, and the gorge in which it lies, has a very pretty, neat, and cheerful appearance, as seen from the summit. The fortifications, with which the hill is crowned, are admirably constructed, and completely command the anchorage and the town.

Leaving Ladder Hill, the road winds a little east of south, over low hills, and through majestic prickly pears, dwarf junipers, and scattered forests of firs; among which may be seen flocks of sheep, goats, and swine, with vast numbers of domestic fowls feeding on the tender herbage. The surface of the interior is exceedingly uneven. The plains are few, and of small extent. Hills and mountainous peaks are seen on every hand, some of them crowned with the dark and dense foliage of the redwood, stringwood, dogwood, Australian willow, and the cabbage-tree, with its beautiful and showy white blossoms, as large as the cauliflower; while their sides frequently present beautiful slopes of pasture, and patches under cultivation. At short intervals, very tasteful cottages and country seats appear, embosomed in verdure, and surrounded with gardens, whose flowers—among which the beautiful white bells of the moon-plant appear conspicuous—fill the atmosphere with their delicious odors. Occasionally a glimpse is caught, through the deep gorges, and abrupt ravines, and precipitous chasms of the rocky substratum, of the surging ocean dashing against the storm-lashed rocks, and stretching far away to the dim and unvaried horizon. The hedges, by which the farms are bordered, are adorned with a pleasing variety of wild flowers, while the fields are carpeted with luxuriant grass, in the midst of which the most graceful plants are ever blooming.

Passing over a depression called "Half-Tree Hollow," the road leads across another elevation, known as "Red Hill," and along the base of "High Knoll," which rises on the left 1,903 feet above the sea. From this point, the central portions of the island are seen to great advantage. At a short distance on the left, in a northeasterly direction, romantically situated at the head of the ravine, on which James' Town is built, is the pretty cottage, called "the Briars," where Napoleon took up his temporary abode, the day after his landing, with its owner and occupant, Mr. Balcombe, and remained, secluded from observation, until the premises at Longwood, in the north-eastern quarter of the island, were put in order for his accommodation. Here he dwelt from October 17th to December 9th, 1815, at which time he removed to his future home. The grounds attached to the cottage are about ten acres in extent, and are laid out in beautiful walks and beds of flowers, giving to the place an air of decided comfort and repose, rendered still more lovely by contrast with the arid and irregularly-precipitous rocks of the ravine, which thence finds its way to James' Town and the ocean.

To the right of High Knoll, and of the Sandy Bay Road, stretches off toward the setting sun, a beautiful slope of ground, appropriated to the use of the government. Here is the official residence of his Excellency, the Governor, called "Plantation House." It is a most delightful spot, and cultivated with the greatest care. The grounds are laid out with taste, and adorned with every variety of shrubbery. Some of the choicest shade and fruit-trees of Europe are seen growing here, side by side with the stately palm of India, and other trees of tropical climes. The gardens abound with the most charming flowers, and the house is surrounded by the most pleasing walks and drives. It was the only place which the British government excepted in the selection of a residence for their imperial prisoner.

From the base of High Knoll, the road runs a little to the west of south, and then southerly to an elevation called "Sandy Bay Ridge," which overlooks the valley of Sandy Bay on the south. Far away to the east, "Diana's Peak" lifts its majestic head to the heavens, and attains the height of 2,700 feet, overlooking, in its peerless elevation, every other point on the island, and commanding an uninterrupted prospect of the boundless ocean, north, east, south, and west. From the sides of this mountain, are seen oozing out, in numerous places, cooling streams of the purest and sweetest water, spreading fertility over the island, and refreshing, not only the residents, but the thousands of mariners who resort hither for supplies. The prospect, by moonlight, from the sides of the mountain, is spoken of with delight by every visitor. So clear and bright is the light of the moon, as to make it easy to read the smallest print. All along the base of the mountain, in the valley, grows the pure white Egyptian lily, called the calla. Seen by the silvery light of a South Atlantic moon, these callas appear like starry spots on the verdant plain; and the beholder seems to stand between two firmaments, above and below, in mid-heaven.

In passing over Sandy Bay Ridge, whose summit rises a short distance from the road, the visitor leaves on the right, at a somewhat greater distance, toward the southwestern extremity of the island, another elevated point called "High Peak," but little inferior to Diana's Peak. It is the termination of a calcareous ridge, which stretches across the island from east to west, dividing it into two unequal parts. The northern portion is much the largest, and the most valuable. It embraces, interspersed with curious and romantic knolls and hills, besides the valley of James' Town and Plantation House already described, the Plain of Longwood, Rupert's Valley, the crater-like dell, called "The Devil's Punch-bowl," "Lemon Valley," and other interesting spots, where the principal residents have built their country residences, and where they live in an almost perpetual summer, or rather spring. The southern portion of the island is much less extensive. The range of hills, which border it on the north, slope somewhat abruptly to the south, and overlook a most lovely rolling valley, famed for its coffee plantations, extending about four miles from east to west, and about two miles in breadth, to the rock-bound shore of the Atlantic. It is the valley of Sandy Bay. The latter is the only spot on the southern shore, from which the interior of the island can be reached. It was, therefore, put under the closest scrutiny by the government, during the confinement of Napoleon, and the approach guarded by frowning batteries.

The descent to this valley is not easily accomplished. The road winds around the sides of the precipitous hills, and in many places is both steep and dangerous. But the visitor is amply compensated for his occasional fears, and the fatigue of his journey, by constant developments of the ever-changing loveliness of the scenery.

At the hospitable dwelling of Mr. Lambe, Mr. Bertram and his companion received a hearty welcome, and soon obtained the consent of himself and wife to the proposition for holding religious services at their house. They had recently erected a new edifice for their own use, which was yet hardly finished. A part of this house, it was arranged, was to be open statedly for the worship of God, and the accommodation of the inhabitants of that section of the island, who could be induced to attend upon the ministrations of the word of God. The house was built on a rocky elevation, at the left of a singular conical mountain, a thousand feet high, called "Old Lot," and about a mile to the east of another group, called "Lot's Wife, and her Children." Adjacent to the house is a fine garden, where, beneath the fig-trees, peach-trees, guava-trees, and majestic bananas, or plantains, the visitors walked or reclined in the refreshing shade, and partook of the pleasant and excellent fruit.

The first sermon ever preached in Sandy Bay Valley, was delivered by Mr. Bertram, on a Thursday evening, at the house of Mr. Lambe, on the occasion of the visit just described. From that time forward, he ordinarily preached at Sandy Bay, once or twice every week; generally on Thursday evening, and every Sabbath afternoon. Afterward, when Mr. Janisch began to preach, service was also held there every Sabbath morning.

The effort thus happily begun, was attended by the Divine favor, and followed with His blessing. The poor neglected population of this remote valley, for whose spiritual welfare none had cared, were grateful to the missionary for his kind services, and flocked to hear the word with delight. Not a few of them were led to see their need of a Saviour, and to cry to God for mercy.

But no sooner was it known that the despised band of dissenters were beginning to spread themselves over the island, and to carry the message of salvation to its farthest shores, than the sticklers for "the Church" were seized with alarm. All at once they made the discovery that there were souls to be cared for in the secluded valleys of St. Helena. At the entrance of Sandy Bay Valley is a school-room, most eligibly located for a place of worship. Mr. Bertram had applied to the authorities for permission to use it, as occasion offered, for the worship of God, but had been denied. Very soon, however, after he had begun to preach at Mr. Lambe's house, one of the parochial clergymen made arrangements for a stated religious service at this very school-room, and at the very hour when Mr. Bertram usually preached. As the people, in their simplicity, preferred to go where they could learn the way of salvation, and have their hearts warmed with longing desires after God and heaven, although they were warned of the awful danger of schism, and told to beware of the damning sin of setting up another altar, and substituting a conventicle for the church of God, the liturgy was often read in the hearing of a very small and uninterested audience. Pains were, therefore, taken by some of the adherents of "the Church," to station individuals "in the ways," and to accost the natives, as they passed along to Mr. Lambe's house, with entreaties, promises, warnings, and threats, to induce them to forsake the schismatical preacher, and show themselves good Christians and churchmen, by joining with the congregation at the school-room. This course of conduct, so intolerant and sectarian, so worthy of scorn and reprobation by every true follower of Christ, was applauded by the Church party and their priests, as evidence of the piety and zeal of their bigoted adherents.

To carry forward this opposition, required more exertion than the two chaplains, so long used to the easy, quiet way of their class, were willing to put forth. An assistant was needed. Word must be sent to England that the Church is in danger, and another full-fledged Tractarian clergyman must be sent out, not only to preach on the Sabbath to the natives, but to lecture during the week, to keep a school for instruction in the higher branches of learning, and to visit the poor. Public meetings were called, and a sufficient salary readily subscribed by the officials, and the zealous churchmen of the town.

Several months passed, and the long-expected Oxonian arrived. Great was the expectation, and loud the exultation, of the party in power, at the success of their application. This new successor of the apostles, or rather, candidate for the succession, was quite a curious specimen of clerical sufficiency. Dressed according to the latest Oxford fashion, in the cut of the ecclesiologistical school, he stepped on shore, and very condescendingly suffered himself to be escorted by some of the residents to the lodgings that awaited him in his new home. Whether short-sighted in reality, as his frequent use of an eye-glass would indicate, or not, he certainly proved himself exceedingly short-sighted in leaving the academical shades of old Oxford for the tropical sky of James' Town.

It was soon found, that he had no more disposition than his two elder brethren in the priesthood, to make himself one of the people, to go out into the highways and hedges, the lanes and alleys, and gather in guests for the gospel-supper, to instruct the young in useful knowledge, or to preach the acceptable year of the Lord. He could read the liturgy with a grace, and pronounce "a beautiful, pious sermon" of some fifteen or twenty minutes' length ; he knew all the attitudes and gestures, and could display a jeweled finger, and a lily-white hand to admiration, but nothing further in the way of winning souls. The subscribers to the salary, and the petitioners to "my Lord" of London, were alike mortified. They had evidently "paid too dear for the whistle." A brief period sufficed to convince this scion of Oxford that he was out of his place, and to determine him to leave St. Helena to her own fate. Great was the relief to the instigators of the Quixotic undertaking, when their hero bade farewell to "the Rock of the Ocean," and returned the way that he came, to expatiate in a wider field, and in more hopeful circles of society.

These anti-evangelical movements were not entirely without their designed effect. Some, who at first came to hear Mr. Bertram, and appeared to be interested in his preaching, withdrew from his meetings. Some were intimidated by threats of being discarded from service, and others were flattered with the attentions of those to whom they had been wont to look up as to beings of a superior order. The minds of some were staggered for a time, and they knew not what to believe.

But this state of uncertainty did not long continue. Prayer, unceasing, was offered to God; and, in season and out of season, Mr. Bertram and his brethren labored to pour the light of eternal truth into the darkened understandings of these perishing islanders. Their prayers were heard; their labors were not in vain. The word of God took effect. One and another began to weep for sin, and to cry, "What shall I do to be saved?" The showers of divine grace began to descend. The well-watered seed began to spring up, and bear fruit to the glory of God. The gracious influences were diffused throughout the valley; until scarcely a house could be found, in that part of the island, in which there was not some one soul rejoicing in hope of the glory of God; while in some habitations, two, three, and even more were raising their songs together in praise of redeeming love. Many of these were wonderful trophies of grace. From among the most unpromising and hopeless hearers of the word, it pleased God to select the subjects of His saving love. "The publicans and the harlots" believed, when the proud and self-righteous Pharisee rejected the humbling doctrines of the lowly Jesus. And so it was at Sandy Bay.

During the progress of this work of grace, in the early part of 1848, the island was visited by the Rev. Jonathan Wade and his wife, missionaries of the "American Baptist Board for Foreign Missions," who had been laboring, since December, 1823, in connection with the now sainted Judson, in Burmah. Their stay was prolonged, by the will of God, for the space of three months. Mr. Wade very gladly entered with Mr. Bertram into the delightful service of directing the awakened sinner to the Lamb of God; and greatly was his kind assistance prized. "We witnessed," he says, "the first baptisms administered there. A church was established, and sixty believers were added to it during the three months of our stay with them."

The faithfulness of these converts has been fairly tested. Few, if any, have gone back to the world, or brought reproach upon the cause of Christ. Their zeal for the worship of God is worthy of all praise and imitation. Nothing but the hand of God can keep them from the place of prayer. In all weathers, by day and by night, when the bright moon sheds her clear light on their path, or when the earth, in her absence, is shrouded in darkness, they will thread their way through the deep gorges, and along the shelving paths of the beetling cliffs, where a foreigner would not dare to trust his foot, or even a domesticated goat venture to climb, and reach the place where the word of God is to be preached, in season to unite in the opening exercises of public worship.

The success, which crowned this first attempt to extend the dissenting interest beyond the immediate neighborhood of James' Town, prompted Mr. Bertram and his brethren to find other places for the preaching of the gospel. "FRANCIS PLAIN," lies but a short distance south of "The Briars," having "Halley's Mount" on the northeast, "Alarm-house Mount," on the southeast, and "High Knoll" on the west. It occupies nearly the exact center of the island, and is surrounded by noble scenery. A station was commenced at this point, not long after the one at Sandy Bay was established. Here, too, the word took effect. A worthy matron, residing at "Rose Bower," in the neighborhood of Francis Plain, toward the northeast, with her lovely family, frequently attended on Mr. Bertram's preaching;

and the eldest two of her daughters were soon brought to trust in Jesus Christ for salvation and eternal life.

But it soon became evident that Mr. Bertram was not wanted at Francis Plain. The door was closed against him and his brethren ; not, however, until " a great door and effectual" had been opened for him at Rose Bower, by Him who "openeth and no man shutteth." At this station, a regular service was speedily established, and every Lord's Day the word of God has since been proclaimed. God has owned His people, heard their prayers, and poured out His Spirit. A mixed congregation of whites and native islanders, not large at the commencement, as the population was limited, but constantly increasing, have continued to assemble here for instruction in holy things ; and a goodly number of them have turned to the Lord.

Attempts had been made by Mr. Bertram, previous to this last arrangement, to establish preaching stations both at Longwood, the residence of Napoleon, and Sane Valley, the place of his burial; but not meeting with sufficient encouragement, Rose Bower was fixed upon, as being nearly central to Francis Plain, and these two localities; and as affording sufficient facilities for all in this part of the island who desired to attend.

Sane Valley is about three and a half miles

from James' Valley, and was selected by Napoleon himself as the place for his sepulchre. It is a quiet and romantic dell, at some little distance from the road, approached by a circuitous and somewhat precipitous path, overhung by yews, cedars, and weeping willows. A well of pure and delicious water springs up about ten or fifteen yards from the tomb, where the Chinese domestics of the Emperor were wont to fill their silver pitchers, which they carried to Longwood for the use of their master. It is said to be the best water on the island. Hither, also, Napoleon frequently resorted for recreation and repose—sometimes alone, and at other times with Madame Bertrand for his companion. "Here," he had said, "if I die on this island, I wish to be buried." And here his mortal remains were deposited, with military honors, on the 8th of May, 1821, in a plain vault, about eight feet in length, three in breadth, and seven in depth. The tomb is inclosed by a plain iron railing, about ten feet square, and overhung by a willow-tree, now almost leafless and branchless, by reason of the Vandal ravages of visitors, who have borne it away piece-meal as memorials of the illustrious exile. A few small cedars are planted around it.

In this beautiful and secluded retirement, the body of the Emperor was suffered to repose until the 15th of October, 1840, exactly twenty-five years from the day that he arrived at St. Helena; when, by arrangement between the French and British governments, it was exhumed, with much parade, under the direction of the Prince de Joinville, and placed on board of the Belle Poule frigate, to be conveyed to France. It was found in a state of excellent preservation, in consequence of the admirable manner in which it had been embalmed by the French physicians. It now reposes under the dome of the magnificent "Hotel des Invalides," at Paris, where it was deposited with immense pomp and ceremony, on the 15th of December, 1840, in a marble tomb, that has already cost the French nation more than six millions of francs.

A poor widow, Mrs. Torbet, occupies a cottage about thirty yards from the tomb, who rents the grounds from the government, and collects from the visitors the sum of one dollar, for which she also furnishes refreshments to such as wish them. A superannuated British sergeant, also, lives near, who has had the charge of the tomb ever since it received the imperial remains, to whom it is customary also to give a shilling for the information which he prides himself in giving with the greatest accuracy.

Longwood is but a short distance beyond Sane Valley, but cannot be reached in a direct route. It is approached by a good road, some two miles in length, nearly level, running along the top of a barren ridge, Rupert's Valley being in full view on the left, and the beautiful valley leading to Levelwood on the right. On either hand, deep and inaccessible gullies are passed, to which have been given such names as the "Devil's Gorge," etc. Longwood is the largest plain on the island, comprising, inclusive of Deadwood, about fifteen hundred acres of fertile land, sloping toward the southwest. The name was given on account of the extent of wood formerly found here. The house, originally the residence of the lieutenant-governor, is elevated one thousand seven hundred and sixty-two feet above the sea. It is the highest table-land on the island, and, in consequence, is less subject to heat than almost any other residence, enjoying a pure air and bracing atmosphere, as well as an extensive prospect. The grounds are adorned with dense patches of shrubbery, and the herbage has a peculiarly fresh and verdant appearance, by reason of its exposure to the balmy and grateful sea-breezes. The house is surrounded with tasteful pleasure-grounds, and has on the northeast a spacious common, covered with a rich carpet of the finest wire-grass, and pleasantly shaded, at appropriate distances, with the luxuriant gum-tree. It is approached from the road through an avenue of pine and gum-trees, the branches of which are hung with a drooping moss. The plain is bounded on the east and west by conical hills, giving a pleasing and romantic character to the scenery. "Flag-staff Hill," which overlooks the plain on the west, attains an elevation of twenty-two hundred and seventy-two feet above the sea. The grounds extend on the northeast to the rocky barrier against which the ocean-waves are for ever breaking. The place is entirely secluded from the other portions of the island, and afforded the Emperor abundant opportunities of walking, or riding on horseback or in his carriage, over a space of twelve miles in circuit, unattended and uninterrupted. Beyond these bounds he could also go at pleasure, under the escort of a British officer. Every indulgence was granted him compatible with the entire security of his person.

The house itself, though by no means handsome, or having any pretensions to architectural beauty—a low, one-story building, in the form of an L—had been fitted up with all the conveniences of which it was capable, and was well suited to a gentleman of rank living in retirement. In the year 1816, the materials and furniture for a new house were sent at great expense from England, but, owing to the difficulty of ascertaining from Napoleon how he would have the materials used, much delay occurred in the erection; so that, ere it was finished, he was too unwell to be removed to it. It was built of yellow sand-stone, one story in height, contains a handsome suite of rooms, and is some hundred yards to the northwest from the old house, compared with which it is quite a palace. The Emperor's residence and grounds are now held by Captain Mason, a retired army officer, who rents the place from the government, and exacts half a dollar, or two shillings sterling, from every visitor. The house is now but little better than a barn, with broken glass, and disfigured walls, unoccupied except by fowls, and as a stable in one portion of it. It seems to have undergone no repairs for thirty years. The new building is occupied by some one or more of the British officers, to whom is committed the charge of the magnetic observatory, the instruments being erected in a detached building.

The population of this portion of the island, it will thus be seen, is very limited, and furnishes but little inducement for the establishment of a preaching station in the neighborhood. The few families at Longwood and Sane Valley can all very easily attend, if they will, upon the services at Rose Bower.

Thus, in the good providence of God, Mr. Bertram was furnished with great opportunities for usefulness at St. Helena. Three preaching stations had been established, and a church gathered, to which constant accessions were made from month to month. The work grew upon his hands, and demanded more time and strength than he could possibly devote to it. Once or twice he was brought low by severe illness. When the Rev. Mr. Jamieson, a missionary of the Presbyterian Board, stopped at the island in the summer of 1846, on his way from India, he found Mr. Bertram suffering from a severe affection of the throat, which prevented his preaching for some considerable time. To the eminent skill, and assiduous attentions of his excellent physician, John Stewart, M.D., he was placed under great obligations, during his illness and recovery. The impaired state of his health compelled him to seek a residence in the country. A snug cottage was found at Sandy Bay, near Mr. Lambe's house, which he has since occupied at least a portion of the year.

During his illness, his place was in part supplied by his young friend, Hudson R. Janisch, whose profiting had appeared to all. The superior talents and education of Mr. Janisch so manifestly fitted him, together with his ardent piety, to be a helper to Mr. Bertram in the ministry, that, after a season of preparatory study, he was ordained, April 2d, 1848, to the ministry of the gospel, on the occasion of the Rev. Jonathan Wade's visit to the island. He has proved himself a worthy coadjutor of his spiritual father, and been of the utmost service to the church in many respects. God has owned his labors ; and, by means of his preaching, not a few have turned to the Lord.

Two of the brethren, James Elliott, one of the few who had been converted previous to Mr. Bertram's arrival, and Thomas Charlett, were elected and ordained to the office of the eldership, both of whom have proved themselves faithful and valiant soldiers of the Cross. The former, having exhibited a good degree of talent in the exercise of his spiritual gifts, was licensed to preach and exhort in public worship. At the close of 1849, more than one hundred souls had been hopefully converted, and added to the Church. Two other brethren, George F. Milne and Thomas Dick, have been licensed to give a word of exhortation among the people.

Schools, also, have been established under the influence and by the enterprise of this humble body of dissenting Christians, which are accomplishing much good. They have Sunday schools, containing about two hundred scholars, at James' Town, Sandy Bay, Half-Tree Hollow, and Level-wood. Day schools also have been opened in the town and at Sandy Bay, in which from eighty to one hundred children are taught.

The poor natives, as well as the imported Africans, for whom almost nothing had ever before been done, in the matter of preparing them for death and the judgment, have many of them been brought under the influence of these schools, and the preaching of the word, by which some of them have been led to Christ. Much praise is due also to the benevolent Mr. Thompson, (whose school-room was obtained for Mr. Bertram soon after his arrival,) for his humanity to the Africans of St. Helena. For several years he has sought to give them the advantages of education, and taught many of them by night in a school that he opened for the purpose. The blessings of the poor African will long rest upon him for these labors of love.

The condition of these Africans is fitted to awaken in their behalf the deepest sympathy and commiseration. They have, the greater part of them, been rescued from slavers, on the coast of Africa, or on the middle passage, and brought into St. Helena by the British armed cruisers. About a mile to the east of James' Valley, and parallel with it, is a similar ravine, or gorge, of about the same width, extending some two or three miles into the interior, called "Rupert's Valley." It has been appropriated by the government to the use of the liberated Africans, who are brought to the island in these slave-ships. As soon, of course, as they touch the soil of the island, they are free.

It is an awfully horrid sight to witness the unlading of one of these slave-ships. When brought out from between decks, where they have been packed together, men, women, and children, in a state of almost entire nudity, in the midst of their own filth, destitute of air, and almost suffocated with the terrible stench, they are scarcely able, in many cases, to crawl, much less to stand; so emaciated and enfeebled have they become, in consequence of the dreadful fevers and other diseases to which their confinement and treatment have subjected them. When brought on shore, they are laid out on the ground in rows, crying, as well as their strength will permit, in the most doleful accents, "*Vava! vava!*" Water! water!

Hundreds and thousands of them perish, notwithstanding all the care that is taken of them after they land. The whole valley has in consequence become a "valley of dry bones." The sick are placed in hospitals, built on an elevated ridge overlooking the valley on the east, and have medical attendance; the naked are clothed, and the hungry fed. In the course of about six weeks those of them that survive the inhuman treatment of the slavers, and the infernal horrors of the middle passage, are sent over to the West India islands, to find employment. Some of them remain on the island, when there is a demand for labor. To send them back to Africa again, would be to subject them once more to capture and slavery.

If any apologist for slavery could see what Mr. Bertram has seen in Rupert's Valley, and what may be seen there month after month, and year after year, and still continue to uphold a system conceived in the very depths of iniquity, fraught with all the evils that can be heaped upon poor down-trodden humanity, and sustained by the most diabolical cruelty, he must have a heart lost to all sense of justice, of pity, and of humanity. It is the most horrid system ever devised by men or devils for the eradication of God's image from man, and the conversion of human beings into brutes, on the one hand, and on the other, fiends incarnate. "How long, O Lord! how long," shall the accursed traffic be supported by the toleration of the system in Christian lands? How long shall Ethiopia stretch out her hands to God, and cry for pity and compassion? Speed, oh, speed the day, when the shackles shall fall from the last slave on earth, and the day of universal freedom shall shed its blissful light on every habitation of man!

Previous to August 1st, 1834, when the British Emancipation Act, by which every slave in the empire was declared free, went into force, slavery existed on the island in a mild form. During the administration of Sir Hudson Lowe, and while

Napoleon was on the island, a regulation was voluntarily adopted by the citizens, at a public meeting, held August 13th, 1818, by which it was provided, that all children born of a slave mother, from and after the next Christmas, should be free; the boys to be apprenticed to the proprietors of the parent until eighteen, and the girls until sixteen years of age. Through the benevolent exertions, principally, of Mr. Bertram and his associates, these freed men and their families, who constitute the native population already described, are gaining instruction in matters pertaining to their moral and religious duties, and making creditable advances in the various pursuits of industry, by which they are rapidly rising to their proper rank in society.

Reference has already been made, on a previous page, to the work of grace which, shortly after the commencement of this mission at James' Town, prevailed among the soldiers of the garrison. Not a few of these hardy, and, too often, profane and dissolute, sons of war were brought, from year to year, to enlist under the banner of the great "Captain of their Salvation;" and become each of them "a good soldier of Jesus Christ."

Shortly after the opening of the mission-house, a theatre was attempted in the barracks, directly across the street, and opened on the same evenings of the week on which the dissenting chapel was opened. The attention of the soldiers was thus diverted or distracted from the preaching of the word. Of course, every inducement was held out, to draw a full audience, to witness the stage-playing, both from the garrison and the town. The introduction of a species of amusement which has ever proved a fruitful means or occasion of dissipation and uncleanness, as well as an effectual source of hardness of heart, and blindness of mind, was a great grief to the little band of brethren, who were laboring for the salvation of the souls of their fellow-sinners. It was regarded as one of the greatest obstacles to the success of their heavenly work.

But though "troubled on every side," they were "not distressed—perplexed, but not in despair." They knew that the cause was God's, and must prevail. "Prayer," therefore, "was made without ceasing of the church unto God," that this hindrance might be removed. Month after month they prayed, until "the Lord hearkened and heard." The hearts of God's people were at length gladdened by the sight of Sergeant Noble among the penitents, crying for mercy and confessing his sins. Soon after Sergeant Wright also was seen bowing his head like a bulrush before the gales of grace from the heavenly world. They had both been among the foremost in the support and management of the theatre, as well as in their opposition to religion. But now they became illustrious trophies of redeeming love, and gave themselves with all their hearts to the service of Christ. The operations of the theatre were suspended, and the gospel triumphed gloriously. At a subsequent period the theatre was again opened—bût it pleased God once more to stretch out His hand, and bring their stage-manager, Cluney, of the army, to bow at the feet of Jesus. Such manifestations of the power of the gospel, not only encouraged the hearts of Mr. Bertram and his brethren to pray and labor in hope, but carried conviction also to the minds of the careless and the profane, of whom not a few were brought to hear and believe.

It was not, however, without many and severe trials arising from domestic bereavement, (the death of his youngest son, August 22, 1848,) and pecuniary embarrassments, that Mr. Bertram was enabled to prosecute his benevolent and useful plans. A very heavy burden was devolved upon the humble brethren, who had clustered about him, in the purchase of their mission-house, the payment of the annual interest on the mortgage with which the property was incumbered, and the support of their pastor and his family. They were not, as has been seen, of the wealthier classes, and but few of them able to advance much on the necessary expenses of their households. Yet what they could do, they did freely and gladly. Their pastor could truly say of them, as Paul said of the Corinthians, that "the abundance of their joy and their deep poverty (in some cases,) abounded unto the riches of their liberality. For to their power I bear record, yea, and beyond their power, they were willing of themselves, praying us with much entreaty that we would receive the gift."

It will be borne in mind, that, when the agreement was made in August, 1845, for the mission premises, it became necessary to wait for the ratification of the contract by the owner, who resided in the East Indies. Several months elapsed before an answer could be received. The state of the treasury of the infant enterprise, when at length the arrangement was completed, may be seen from the following letter, written by a member of the congregation, in the early part of June, 1846, to a friend in Cape Town, which appeared in the columns of the Cape Magazine for August, 1846:

"You are aware that a house and premises have been hired for the chapel. The situation is, I think, decidedly the most eligible the town affords; the lower part of the house was thrown into one. It is a commodious place of worship, sufficiently large for the congregation usually assembling there. The mission-box, monthly collections, and subscriptions of some few individuals, pay the current expenses, and afford Mr. Bertram £150 per annum, a small and straitened income in this *expensive* place. His hearers consist almost wholly of the very poor; so that it seems wonderful that even this much is effected. But no surplus remains when the necessary and current expenses are paid. When the preparation, or building, of a mission house was first proposed, persons put down their names for various sums, together amounting to nearly £300. Upon the strength of this, the committee of management, too sanguine in their expectations, offered to purchase the premises now occupied for £550; £300 to be paid down, the remaining £250 in installments. The owner of the premises being in India, it became necessary for her agent to write for her sanction to this proposal. An answer of acceptance has now arrived; but, alas! there are no funds. Another purchaser is ready to pay down the whole amount, anxious to procure the premises for a far different purpose, and if the committee cannot lay down the £300 within six months, the opportunity is lost. Without aid, and liberal aid, too, from the Cape, I fear there is no possibility of obtaining the necessary amount. Mr. Bertram has strong faith that the Lord will send help in time of need, and some of the community here are deeply anxious, and much engaged in prayer for its accomplishment. And, much as, we know, there is to occupy the attention of Cape friends, we yet hope that you will not desert us. Sums amounting to £60 are sure, I believe; but what is that to £300? If I were at the Cape, I would beg from door to door for the cause, rather than see it fail. The evident blessing that has attended, and still attends, Mr. Bertram's labors in this benighted spot, is such as proves him to be sent of God; and therefore I believe it will prosper; it must succeed."

An appeal to the friends of the Redeemer at Cape Town was prefixed to the letter as it appeared in print, and followed by another in the Magazine for September. In this latter, it was stated, that the "opposition, which ever attends the doctrines of the Cross when boldly and faithfully preached, threatens to deprive this flock of the place of worship that has been provided."

Although it was a season of great commercial depression in the colony of the Cape of Good Hope, the sum of forty-two pounds, of which thirty were contributed by four individuals, Messrs. Hawkins, M'Leod, Alexander and A. Steedman, was presently obtained, and forwarded to St. Helena.

In the "First Report of the Christian Mission from the Cape of Good Hope to St. Helena," presented at a public meeting in the mission house at James' Town, December 29th, 1849, and which was presently published in pamphlet form, the state of the funds is spoken of as follows:

"The purchase of the mission house had been now effected for the sum of £550, payable in four years with interest; two of which have now elapsed. But the yearly installments, resting principally on a few, have indeed been trying, uphill work. Four of the brethren have subscribed for this special purpose £27 10s. a year each, and for the rest we have sometimes been driven to our wits' end, not knowing how or where to turn. Every way blocked up, and apparently every avenue closed, Moses-like we have stood still to see the salvation of God. The great sea of difficulty has divided in the midst. A friend has stepped forward; relief has appeared. A Solomon has once and again stretched out his hand. A Scott, with others who have always thought they had a right to do what they thought proper with their own, have kindly lent their aid; and for which, in this public report, we beg to express our grateful sense. To help us temporally, God has hitherto said 'to the north, Give up, and to the south, Keep not back.' At Jehovah's bidding, Christian sympathy has been excited; holy benevolence has stretched out her lovely, helping hand. Cape Christianity hath not forgotten to make her collection for the poor saints, in behalf of this infant cause of God on this rock of the ocean. Christian friends and gentlemen at the Cape, in the spirit of the glorious gospel, free from all sectarian bigotry, subscribed their names and put down their consecrated pounds to aid us in our time of need. The enemy felt our new strength and feared, and the weak said, we are strong. Our prayer to God is that He may reward those our kind donors a hundred-fold, and that those acts of Christian benevolence may not be forgotten in the day of the Lord Jesus.

"In consequence of this yearly installment for the mission house purchase, and other incidental expenses arising from the lighting and cleaning, Mr. Bertram has been but scantily supported."

At the expiration of four and a half years, a debt of three hundred pounds (fifteen hundred dollars) still remained, for which the mission premises were mortgaged. In the circumstances in which the congregation were placed, it was very desirable that this burden should be removed. In addition, moreover, to this demand, the providence of God was evidently calling upon them to erect a house of worship for the accommodation of the residents in Sandy Bay Valley, on the opposite side of the island; and another in the neighborhood of Rose Bower, in the very heart of the island. Both of these stations had now become centers of a most salutary influence, and could not be dispensed with. Hitherto they had been under the necessity of meeting, for public worship, in the private houses of the two friends, whose hearts God had opened to receive His word and His ministers.

To effect these objects, application must be made for foreign aid. It was not to be obtained on the island. The congregation had strained every nerve to meet the current expenses of the enterprise thus far, and had done nobly. A great work had been accomplished in a very short period. Out of themselves they could look for but little sympathy among the wealthier classes of St. Helena, who were mostly connected with, or dependent for patronage upon, the government; and so under the influence of the colonial Church.

In this state of things, after much deliberation and prayer, it was determined, to make an appeal to the friends of the Redeemer in the more favored portions of His vineyard. The health of Mr. Bertram, by reason of the incessant labors to which he had cheerfully devoted himself for the past five years, had now become somewhat impaired. A season of rest, or recreation, it was thought, such as a long sea-voyage, and a visit to Great Britain and America, would afford, might recruit his waning strength, and refit him for resuming, with increased vigor, the delightful work of evangelizing the native population of St. Helena.

Nor was such an appeal to be regarded alone in the light of asking alms. St. Helena is the half-way house on the high road from the shores of the North Atlantic to the East Indies. The merchants and the missionaries of Great Britain and America find it a most convenient and welcome stopping-place, on their way home from an Indian residence. To those of them, whose health has been sacrificed to the purposes of commerce, or of the gospel, it is indeed most refreshing to find, in the midst of the weary waste of waters, such a convenient haven, and so delightful a climate, where to tarry a few days or weeks, amid healthful and balmy breezes, on their homeward way. Mr. Bertram and his brethren had been accustomed, year by year, to extend the hand of fellowship and welcome to the weary, worn-out missionary, and to cheer him in his feebleness and sorrow, as the following testimonial, from the pen of the Rev. Jonathan Wade, makes abundantly evident:

"Both the Baptist and Pædo-Baptist denominations, having missionaries in the East, owe these St. Helena disciples a large debt already; and this debt will increase every year. Their missionaries, who are returning home in feeble health, mostly call at the island; and, but for the hospitality of the members of this church, would be obliged to pay a guinea a day for board. Mrs. Wade and myself shared their hospitalities during three months, which enabled us to board there at an expense which our usual salary would cover. Brother Bertram and his family vacated his own house for the accommodation of Brother Haswell (Baptist missionary at Amherst, in Burmah) and his family, when they were detained some three or four weeks on the island. Other missionaries, now in this country, have shared their hospitalities for a longer or shorter period."

Thus actuated and encouraged, "the Christian Brethren of the Missionary Church in the Island of St. Helena," as they style themselves, prepared to part for a season with their pastor, and to send him abroad with their salutations and entreaties for help in the good work of the Lord. Relying on the ministerial services of the Rev. Mr. Janisch, and the three licentiates, Elliott, Dick, and Milne, to supply them, in the absence of Mr. Bertram, with spiritual ministrations, they committed him and his beloved family to the guidance of the Great Head of the Church. The farewell services took place at the mission house, on the 18th of February, 1850; on which occasion they mingled their tears with their petitions, and pastor and people wept together at the prospect of separation.

It was an occasion of the deepest interest. Only about four and a half years had elapsed since the lone missionary had set foot on this "Rock of the Ocean," unknown to every inhabitant of the island, and altogether uncertain as to the reception that awaited him. No missionary society had taken him under its patronage, and pledged him a support. He was destitute entirely of all earthly dependence for his daily bread. A single letter to a tradesman, whom he had never seen or known before, was his only passport to favor. His coming had not been heralded in the periodicals of the Cape or the Island, so as to attract the attention of the great, the honorable, and the rich; nor was there a waiting church or religious society, anxiously expecting the arrival of a pastor. Of all the residents on the island, not more, perhaps, than four or five individuals had ever known, by sweet experience, the blessedness of vital piety. Professors there were, and two of them, priests also; but they pertained to the Church of England, were attached to the formalities of a heartless system of religion, and gave but doubtful, if any, evidence of being any thing more than mere nominal Christians. But, whatever they were, he had nothing to expect from them, but discouragement and resistance in every practicable form, to the purpose and aim of his mission.

But now how great a change had been effected! A fond and admiring church (numbering at present about two hundred members) had been gathered around him ; the word of God had been preached in every quarter of the island; preaching stations had been established in town and country; weekly meetings for prayer and the study of the Scriptures had been set up ; Sunday schools and day schools had been gathered, or were soon to be started; the fruitful soil had been plentifully sown with the good seed, and a blessed harvest of souls was springing up all around him, portions of which were already ripe for the sickle. Well might he and his grateful brethren exclaim, in view of these unspeakable mercies, "This is the Lord's doing, and it is marvelous in our eyes."

APPPENDIX.

A.

Very shortly after Mr. Bertram's arrival at St. Helena, he was called to sympathize with the late lamented Adoniram Judson, D.D., in a season of deep affliction. Dr. Judson, in consequence of the alarming state of his wife's health, had been induced to leave his field of labor and his three younger children in Burmah, and to accompany his sinking companion and their three elder children to his native land. They embarked on the "Paragon," for London, April 26th, 1845, about the time that Mr. Bertram arrived at Saldanha Bay. After a brief sojourn at the Mauritius, or Isle of France, of about three weeks, they hastened on their homeward way. Mrs. Judson continued to become more feeble, until the ship came to anchor, at a very early hour in the morning of the 1st of September, in the harbor of James' Town, when, at three o'clock, she closed her earthly pilgrimage. The affecting scenes that followed, are thus related by Mr. Bertram:

"Early in the morning of the 1st of September, I received a note from Mr. Carrol, the American Consul of that island, informing me that a ship, named the Sophia Walker, had dropped anchor in our bay, the previous night, and that she had on board two distinguished passengers, Mr. Judson and lady, with their three children; but, sad to state, since that brief period, Mrs. Judson had departed this life. He further stated, that Mr. Judson sent his christian regards to me, requesting that I would come on board, as he was very desirous to see me. I had heard of Mr. Judson long before, and had learned to think of him as one of the most noble heroes of the 'cross of Christ.' With a heart full of painful sympathy, I hastened to the vessel. As the boat in which I was, neared the floating house of death, I perceived several of the crew approaching the gangway. Deep sorrow was depicted on their countenances. The captain received me with a welcome, and, after a few touching hints, conducted me to the cabin, where I was, for the first time, introduced to Mr. Judson. He held out his hand; but, for a moment, his heart was too full for articulation. He looked pale and careworn. The bitter tears flowed down his cheeks in rapid succession, moistening his lips, as if seeking to find their way back again into that heart of sorrow, whence they flowed. Such a touching scene I never witnessed before. With him stood his three small children, weeping, and refusing to be comforted, because she, whom they so dearly loved, was not. Mr. Judson soon regained his self-possession. He spoke to his afflicted children in the sweetest manner, and in the most consoling language a Christian father's lips could utter, and then turning to me, said,

"'O sir, she died in the Lord—so peacefully. I asked her, but a little before she died, if she loved the Saviour, and could trust her soul into His hands. She answered, "Yes, O yes." Come, Mr. Bertram, will you look at my love? She is just like herself, lovely, even in death.'

"He led the way into the state-room, where lay the cold remains in which once dwelt the soul of her who had given and devoted to the Saviour's cause, her life, her all. Pleasant she was, indeed, even in death. A sweet smile of love seemed to rest on her countenance, as if heavenly grace had stamped it there. Mr. Judson stood at her head, and the children around her, weeping and sobbing. He kissed her cold forehead, again and again, bedewing it with tears.

After a few moments, he said, 'My love suffered much before she died, but never murmured. Her sufferings are over. Yes, she is now in heaven. I did all for her myself; dressed, and laid her out myself. This was her own request. To me it was a painful duty; but God sustained me.'

"He then informed me that arrangements had been made for the funeral, which was to take place at four in the afternoon, and begged I would attend and conduct the religious services on board the vessel. I then left the ship and hastened on shore, to summon all my Christian brethren to be in waiting on the wharf at half past three o'clock. Returning to the vessel, I remained with Mr. Judson until afternoon. When the time for the religious service arrived, the captain called together all the friends who were on board, and all hands who could be spared from the ship. I then read a suitable portion of the Divine word, and gave a brief address—I trust from the Lord a word in season—and then we all knelt in prayer to the wise Disposer of every event. When the service was ended, we again visited the solemn state-room, to take a last look of the departed wife and missionary. The bereaved husband and weeping children fastened their eyes upon the loved remains, as if they could have looked for ever. Weeping, kiss after kiss was imprinted on the cold forehead. The last look was taken, the last kiss imparted, and then all was hid from mortal vision, until the morning of the resurrection. The coffin was removed to the boat which was to convey it on shore. Other boats were connected with this, so arranged as to form a funeral procession—three going ahead, towing the one which contained the corpse, and moving forward with the heavy beatings of their oars, and another followed, in which were Mr. Judson and the three children, with the captain of the ship and myself as chief mourners. Our Christian brethren and sisters were in a goodly number, with Mr. Carrol, the American consul, and his family, and some others of his friends, already waiting on the shore, to join the funeral procession. The body was then transferred from the boat to the bier, which was carried by a number of seamen. The pall-bearers we selected from among our Christian sisters. They were four in number, and chief women, viz., Mrs. Captain O'Connor, of the East India Company; Mrs. Janisch, widow of the late Dutch consul; Mrs. Torbett, of Napoleon's tomb; Mrs. Carrol, American consul's lady. Mr. Judson and myself walked first, leading one of the children; the captain next came, leading the other two; the American consul followed, with his friends; then our Christian brethren and sisters, two and two: the whole numbering about one hundred persons. It is nearly half a mile from the landing to the burying-ground, the way to which lies through the town. The inhabitants paid their respects by closing their shops. The street was considerably lined on either side with spectators, who all appeared to manifest a mournful sympathy with Mr. Judson and the dear children.

"On arriving at the grave, the Episcopal clergyman read the burial service of the Church of England. The body was then committed to its mother dust. Our Christian brethren stood around the grave and sung a solemn hymn, selected for the occasion. During this service, as Mr. Judson stood supported by my arm, I felt his animal frame frequently ready to give way, particularly toward the last, when the coffin was about to be lowered into the grave. I could see him heaving his heart to God, for power from on high, to strengthen him. God heard his prayer, and held him up. All being now over, the Christian friends began to withdraw; but Mr. Judson and the children appeared to linger, as if reluctant to leave the sacred spot. We left the remains of Mrs. Judson in one of the choicest spots of the burying ground—a banian tree spreading its branches over it, as if to guard the precious treasure which lay interred beneath its shade.

'We then conducted Mr. Judson and the children to the house of Mr. Thomas Alesworth, which stood adjacent to the burying-ground. His large parlor was filled with Christian friends. A prayer-meeting was held. A goodly number engaged, each and all praying God for comfort and support to His dear servant and his children, in this their time of need. We all took tea together, and spent the remainder of the time in religious conversation, speaking much of Jesus and the resurrection. And now the time of Mr. Judson's departure drew nigh. The captain called, informing him that there was little time to spare, as the ship was to put out to sea again that evening. Mr. Judson then arose and addressed us. He spoke with feelings of the highest gratitude of the Lord's goodness unto him, in sparing him the painful task of burying the remains of his beloved wife in the restless deep; in bringing her to our island, and in giving her a Christian burial, and surrounding him with so many kind friends, who had joined with him in paying the last tribute of respect to her, who to him had proved one of the best of wives, and the most devoted mother. He said he never could have thought God had so many who loved Him on the island, and that he expected, when Mrs. Judson died, to have buried her with the assistance of a few seamen and a small number of sympathizing friends. He thanked us all from his very heart, in the name of the Lord, for our Christian sympathy and kindness to him and his children, praying God to reward us a thousand fold, to bless us as a Christian Church, and requested that we would follow him with our prayers, when on the mighty deep. He then gave Mr. Carrol and myself charge of the grave, and instructions concerning the headstone. He desired me often to give the hallowed spot, where lay the remains of his beloved wife, a friendly look, instead of himself, who would soon be far away from it; but should continue to visit it in the mournful remembrance of his spirit. We accompanied him to the ship, sorrowing with double sorrow, that we should see his face no more in the flesh. Bidding him God speed, we said the last farewell."

B.

CASES OF HAPPY DEATHS AT ST. HELENA.

As an illustration of some of the blessed results of the St. Helena Mission, the following cases of individuals, who have departed this life, after a happy experience of the power of converting grace, are presented to the reader.

Mrs. Burnham, residing at Hutt's Gate, a short distance south of Napoleon's tomb—an aged person, of large family—was hopefully converted in her last sickness, through the instructions of the missionary. Her youngest daughter, Mrs. Edmonds, also, became a subject of divine grace, was baptized, and shortly after fell asleep in Jesus. Mrs. Youl, a young mother, was led to embrace religion on the bed of death, and died rejoicing in her Saviour. Caesar, a native resident of Sandy Bay Valley, became a remarkable trophy of divine grace, and died a triumphant death at the hospital in James' Town.

On one occasion, late at night, a pressing message reached Mr. Bertram, asking him to visit one of the native women in the country, who was lying at the point of death. "I mounted my horse," he says, "and, accompanied by a friend, rode into the interior about three miles. Leaving our horses at Ridge Hill House, in care of Mr. Scott, where I found a couple of Christian friends awaiting me, we wended our way along the rear of Plantation House, the governor's seat, and, entering a dense forest of pines, by a winding and rugged foot-path, we groped along in darkness, toward the midnight hour, quite uncertain of our footing, and frequently stumbling over some unseen obstruction. It was a gloomy walk, and well fitted, in the circumstances, to fill the mind with deep solemnity.

"At length we reached the place of our destination, and were heralded by a faithful watch-dog. A cluster of rude and humble cottages was before us, scarcely visible in the gloom, known as 'Chinatown,' and formerly occupied by a number of Chinamen, who had mostly been removed by death, leaving their dwellings to be occupied by others. Mr. May, the husband of the sick woman, met us at the door with a taper candle, and conducted us to the bedside of the sufferer. Two or three of the native Christian women were present, who had been in attendance upon their afflicted neighbor for some time previously to our arrival. The inhabitants of St. Helena are distinguished for their kind attentions to the sick and afflicted, as many of the strangers who have visited the island can fully testify. Every delicacy, or alleviation, or relief of any description in their power, is furnished with the greatest tenderness and sympathy.

"The sufferer was dozing when I approached her bed; but after a little, she opened her eyes and gazed about. One of the sisters present said to her, 'Would you like to see Mr. Bertram?' 'Oh! yes,' she replied, with great earnestness. 'Do you know me, Mrs. May?' I asked. 'Yes, sir,' she answered, 'and have been waiting, wishfully, to see you before I died.' 'Have you ever attended my preaching?' 'Yes, many a time, both in the town and at Sandy Bay. Before my marriage, I lived at the Bay with Sister Jones. Alic Jones' wife is my sister. While there, I attended your preaching frequently at Mr. Lambe's house. After my marriage, not long since, I removed to this place, where I have been so much afflicted as to be unable to go and hear you.'

"'Have you learned any thing from the preaching that you have heard?' I asked again. 'Much—very much,' she replied; 'I learned my lost and ruined condition as a sinner against God; His goodness, also, in giving a Saviour, and the love of the Saviour in giving Himself a sacrifice for my sins. I often left Mr. Lambe's house with an aching heart, and would weep in secret, among the rocks, over my grievous sins. I lifted up my cries to God for pardon, until at length I found the Saviour precious to my soul. And oh! He is precious to me now. I feel the sweet comforts of His presence. I am not afraid to die—death hath no terrors for me.' Turning her eyes toward the hearers, she exclaimed, 'Oh! my precious Saviour! I long to be with thee. Methinks I see Him now. I feel that I am His, and He is mine.' She then praised God, that ever she had heard His gospel at my lips.

"Prayer was then offered, in which she engaged most fervently, and every heart seemed to be full of adoring gratitude to God for His wonderful grace. She then asked us to sing a hymn with her before we left; and while we were engaged in the holy exercise, the dying convert sung with more than human voice and ecstasy, her clasped hands being raised toward heaven, and her eyes sparkling with a holy radiance. When we had concluded, she sung on, and cried, 'Sing with me—do n't stop—sing more—sing again. Praise the Lord, O my soul!' Thus she continued, until her physical strength was exhausted; and early in the morning, before the dawning of day, her happy spirit was wafted by angels to her Redeemer's bosom.

"Mrs. Young, also, was brought," says Mr. Bertram, "to a saving knowledge of the truth as it is in Jesus, and lived, for two years after her conversion, a most holy and exemplary life. During a painful and lingering illness, she was gloriously sustained by divine grace, and manifested the greatest Christian patience and resignation. Not a murmur was heard to escape from her lips. Often, during her illness, she was filled with 'joy and peace in believing.' She had a faith which took hold and rested upon the imperishable promises of the gospel. As death advanced, her joy increased, her prospects brightened, her tongue was loosed; and, from the abundance of a heart filled with the love of Christ, she spoke at different times to those around her in language more than earthly. She literally died singing the praises of God and of the Lamb.

"Mrs. Gyond had attended Sister Young in all her illness, had heard many faithful warnings, earnest entreaties, and precious invitations to come to the Saviour; and often, during the exercises, had been deeply affected and powerfully awakened; but would again return to folly, until she sat under the sound of another gospel sermon, when she would again melt and quail, and again relapse into her former state of carelessness and indifference for her soul's salvation. But the arrows of God had fastened on her conscience, and rest in her sins was for ever banished from her soul. She struggled for a long time against the truth of God and her own conscience, until she was suddenly seized with a severe illness, when attending her husband at Rose Bower, who was also in a delicate state of health.

"All at once the terrors of death and judgment stared her in the face; the thunders of Mount Sinai's burning and fiery mount carried terror to her quivering soul; she quailed beneath the angry judgment of the Almighty; she felt the value then of a Saviour; and, for refuge, was enabled to flee to the foot of the cross. The family at Rose Bower was pious, and the two eldest daughters, during her illness, daily supplicated for her at a throne of grace. Under their prayers and pious instructions, she was enabled to lay hold of the hope set before her in the gospel; her fears were all subdued, and peace in believing possessed her heart. A short time before her departure, she fell into a doze, from which she awoke in a state of perfect sensibility, giving those around her a most sublime description of a heavenly vision she had seen, sweet music to which she had listened, and holy angels that she had seen. Those, who witnessed her death and all its attendant circumstances, had reason to believe that this was also a brand plucked from the burning.

"Granny Wells, also, an aged woman, converted after she was sixty years of age, exhibited all the glorious evidence of a change of heart. She became an object of universal Christian love among the brethren and sisters on the island. When she could no longer attend the house of God, from feebleness of health and shortness of breath, she had, every Sabbath, a meeting held with her in her own room. This was a sister's meeting, in which numbers regularly engaged in prayer, read the Holy Scriptures, and sang God's praises together. This was Granny Wells's Sabbath-day blessing; nor could her soul, hungering and thirsting after righteousness, ever be satisfied without it. She died in the Lord, in deed and of a truth, beloved by every Christian on the island.

"Sister THOMAS, also, a native, was a glorious example of the converting grace of God. To hear the word of Life, this native would travel over every part of the island, to every missionary station, or preaching place in the town, at Francis Plain, Rose Bower, Sandy Bay, and Longwood, fearing lest she might lose a single gospel sermon. She was a woman of no ordinary mind, and became well instructed in the things of God. Like the woman of Samaria, her zeal to bring others to Christ was manifest in the long journeys she took to different parts of the island, to bring the people under the sound of the glorious gospel, and to win them to Christ. She had wisdom from Heaven to combat error, and to 'contend earnestly for the faith once delivered to the saints.' Both threats and promises were used to draw her from the right way of the Lord; but, with her ears closed, she went on her heavenly course, shouting 'Life, life—eternal life!' She was, however, at times subject to great personal affliction, suffering much from a distemper in the head, which frequently laid her up for days and weeks together. She sickened, at length, for the last time; and, in the triumphs of faith, exchanged this world of suffering and death for the heavenly land, where 'there shall be no more death,' and where 'the inhabitant shall not say I am sick.'

"Mrs. Weston was also brought to a knowledge of the truth as 'it is in Jesus.' She was considerably enlightened and instructed by the preaching of the word at her mother's house at Green Hill, but particularly after her removal to the town, on the bed of affliction, and death. We have good reason to believe that she experienced then a change of heart. She fell asleep in Jesus, in early life, shortly after her marriage. She was accomplished in person and in mind, as well as of a most kind and gentle heart. She was lamented by all on the island. A goodly number of her relatives were brought to the Lord through the preaching of the word, and became members of the mission church. Their consolation was, that she gave good evidence of having found the Lord before her death, and that their painful loss was her eternal gain.

"George M'Nought was born, in the north of Ireland, of Presbyterian parents, and was therefore, to a considerable degree, brought up 'in the nurture and admonition of the Lord.' He had but an imperfect education, could read not very well, and write not much better. He was bred a weaver, and for a time supported himself by his trade; but, being addicted to profanity and dissipation, he at length enlisted as a soldier in her majesty's service, and was sent to St. Helena. He had a fondness for music, and was, in consequence, put in training for the band, into which, after a suitable drilling, he was introduced as a proficient in the art. He was thus elevated above the ranks, and a dress was given him much superior to that of a private. His personal appearance was very attractive; and, by a strict attention to his regimental duties, he won the respect, and secured the approbation, of his officers. But his life, when out of the ranks and the barracks, was very irregular and profane. For two years he continued to pursue a course of high-handed wickedness.

"The soldiers, who had been converted in the revival, were wont to meet at stated times for prayer and conference, in what was called ' the soldiers' room,' attached to the mission premises. This meeting was conducted by Sergeant Brook, a very devoted servant of Christ. These soldiers were animated with an ardent desire for the conversion of their comrades, and frequently singled out one and another as special objects of prayer. At the same time, they endeavored to persuade them to attend upon the preaching of the word.

"Among others, George M'Nought shared in their Christian solicitude, and was at length prevailed upon to enter the house of God, and hear His word. Presently he was awakened to a sense of his guilt, wretchedness, and danger. He was brought to see into what depths of iniquity he had plunged, and how dreadfully wicked and abandoned his life had been. A letter came, just then, from home, in which his godly parents poured forth their affection, in pious counsels and entreaties, urging him to forsake the ways of sin, and turn to the Lord. This timely epistle deepened his conviction, and soon he was led firmly and penitently to resolve, in the strength of the Lord, to seek the mercy of his God, if there was any mercy for such a wretch. Encouraged by his comrades that were pious, who took him by the hand, prayed for, and instructed him, he was brought, under the preaching of the word, to believe with his heart unto righteousness, and to cast the burden of his sins upon his Saviour. His soul was now filled with joy, as one alive from the dead, as a new creature in Christ Jesus. To his anxious parents he sent, in reply, the joyful tidings of the restoration of their prodigal son, and his reconciliation with his offended God and Father.

"He cast in his lot fully with the people of God, and, like Caleb and Joshua, followed the Lord with his whole heart. He was neither a Demas, clinging to this present evil world, nor a Diotrephes, loving the pre-eminence. His was not the Laodicean lukewarmness, nor the Galatian unsteadiness. He counted ' all things but loss' for Christ, set his eyes on the goal, and pressed 'toward the mark, for the prize of the high calling of God in Christ Jesus.' His motto was, 'This one thing I do.' So remarkably did he grow in grace, that all his acquaintances 'took knowledge of him that he had been with Jesus.'

"He abounded and delighted in prayer, spending hours daily with God in the 'soldiers' room' of the mission premises. He shrunk not from the exercise of his gifts in public, and most fervently, as well as effectually, did he pray. It was a great pleasure to all the church to hear him; and rich was the blessing, which seemed always to flow upon them from above, when George prayed.

"He loved the sanctuary, and drank in, with awe and holy reverence, the instructions of God's word, relishing most the strong meat, on which his soul fed and grew apace. He was an example to the believers in the regularity and punctuality of his attendance at prayer and conference meetings, whenever not on regimental duty, as well as on the Sabbath day, to hear the word. His spirituality appeared in his whole deportment, as well as in his speech and devotions. He adored the free, rich, and sovereign grace of God, and greatly delighted in the contemplation of the infinite riches of grace and wisdom that are treasured up in Christ, ever seeking to magnify and exalt the wonders of redeeming love, and to lead his comrades to Jesus. His faith and courage was such, that he could go through fire and water for his beloved Lord. Such, too, was his remarkable proficiency in the knowledge of the truth, as to give undoubted confirmation to the promise, 'All thy children shall be taught of the Lord.'

"Nor was he less distinguished for his humility. Of himself he never spoke, but as 'less than the least' of the saints, and as not worthy to be called a disciple, or to receive even a crumb from the Master's table, or a cup of water from the Lord. If at any time he was troubled with remaining infirmity, he mourned over his corruption, and, with deep contrition.

'At the foot of the cross,
He would weep for his loss,
Till the blood made him holy again.'

"His exertions to lead his comrades to the Saviour were, not only unremitting, but patient and long-continued. He wearied not, nor was he discouraged under rebuke and reproach. He sought them out, entreated and besought them; and not in vain. Many of them were persuaded to accompany him to the sanctuary and the place of prayer, of whom several became happy subjects of grace.

"He delighted, also, in conversing with his fellow Christians on the things pertaining to the kingdom. Often they would gather round him in groups, on the mission premises, and stand, with open mouths and ears, drinking in his homely, yet savory and heavenly talk, by which the sleepy professor was roused, the conscience of the unfaithful stung, the timid encouraged, the feeble strengthened, and the wandering reclaimed. Yet he attempted not to preach or lecture.

"George had been chosen, by reason of his fine person, to be the base-drummer. The carrying of the large drum is very injurious to the chest, and but few persons have been known in the British army who could long sustain the burden. George sank under it, and was under the necessity of leaving the ranks for the hospital. He may have been predisposed to consumption; but the climate of St. Helena had not aggravated the disease, as it is well known to be highly favorable to the removal of such disorders.

"In the hospital he was treated with kindness and skill; so that after some weeks he began to amend, and was permitted to leave the sick room and resume his place in the ranks. During his sickness, he was enabled, by his fervent prayers, pious instructions, and holy conversation, to prove himself a blessing to his fellow patients, some of whom will, through eternity, have occasion to bless God for their acquaintance with him in the hospital.

"Grateful as were his brethren in the church to see him once more among them, it was but for a short season only. His disorder soon became more alarming, and he was obliged to return to the hospital to leave it no more alive. For the space of three months he was gradually sinking, and wasting away; but not a murmuring word escaped his lips. With the utmost patience and resignation he awaited the will of God. He knew 'that all things work together for good to them that love God, to them who are the called according to His purpose.' The language of his heart, as well as of his lips, was, 'Not my will, but thine, be done.' Dearly as he loved life, and clung to it, he would say, 'Though He slay me, yet will I trust in Him.'

"He enjoyed a sweet and serene composure of soul, throughout his illness. Though the 'outward man' was perishing, 'the inward man' was 'renewed day by day.' He rejoiced to do what his wasting strength would allow, for the spiritual welfare of his comrades in affliction. He was visited by many of his fellow Christians, and others also, to all of whom he spake, as he was able, of the worth of the soul, of the necessity of experimental religion, of the willingness of God to save, of the efficacy of a Saviour's blood, of the unspeakable comforts of grace, and the wonderful support of the Spirit. To those who were unconverted, he would speak particularly of the vanities of the world, and the awful danger of dying in sin. 'Ah!' he would say, 'What a miserable, guilty, lost wretch would I be now, had I all the world with me, and no Jesus! How much better am I off, having Christ with me, and but little or nothing of the world. Every day He strengthens me, sustains me, and is preparing me for glory.' Then he would tell of the bright prospect of glory that was spread out before him, and say, 'All this for poor George, unworthy George; not the merited purchase of my own good works; oh! no; but the merited purchase of Jesus' sufferings, precious blood, and death.' He seemed to be completely captivated with the charms of a Saviour's love, and would often repeat those sweet words of Dr. Watts':

'Were the whole realm of nature mine,
That were a present far too small;
Love, so amazing, so divine,
Demands my soul, my life, my all.'

"His Christian brethren, with great modesty, yet with great faithfulness, he would exhort to live near to God, and to fight manfully against the world, the flesh, and the devil. To do this, he told them, they must be stronger in soul than in body—must be strong in the Lord and in the power of His might. To obtain this spiritual 'might in the inner man,' they must give themselves much to private prayer, spend much time with God, and as little as possible with the world. 'Brethren!' he would say, 'Walk with God, and do n't go away from Him; cleave to Him with full purpose of heart, and He will never leave you, never forsake you. I am sure of this. I have tried God for myself; and, notwithstanding all my unworthiness, He has been a God of faithfulness, a promise-keeping God to me. Only see how He is supporting me now! See how He holds me up while heart and flesh is failing me! "The Lord is my portion, saith my soul; therefore will I trust in Him." Oh! when I think of the long-suffering of God to me, and that He spared me, and did not cut me down in my sins; that He sent His servants and His gospel after me, His spirit to quicken, and enlighten, and convert my poor, dead, dark, and guilty soul—oh! the goodness of God to me! "What shall I render unto the Lord for all His benefits toward me?" "Bless the Lord, O my soul, and forget not all His benefits." Oh! brethren, if I get to heaven, I 'll praise Him there as I cannot praise Him here.'

"Thus he would talk to those who visited him day by day—who felt as if they had spent some time on the very suburbs of heaven; and, on meeting some one or another of their friends on the street, after a visit to George, they might be often heard to say, 'Oh! you ought to have heard George, to-day; such heavenly, blessed things he did say! What a blessed state of soul he is in! What a heavenly frame of mind! His heart is full of God. I 'll tell you what it is, the religion that George has is worth more to him now than all the world. Oh! that I may have such religion as George's, when I come to die.' The unconverted, who visited him, all confessed that they saw in him, and heard from him, what they never saw or heard before. He was a subject of discourse all through the town, and all over the island.

"But it became every day more and more apparent, that the day of his departure was at hand—that he was fast ripening for the heavenly kingdom. It was on a dark and drizzly night, and at a late hour of that night, that it came into my mind to visit him. I knew not how, but so it was—the conviction was fastened on my mind, that there would be a change with George before the morning. My family would fain have dissuaded me from visiting the hospital that night, as it was late, wet, and dark. But something said, 'Go, and tarry not.' I left the mission house, and proceeded up the valley, toward the house of mourning. The hospital stands about half a mile above the mission house. It was between the hours of ten and eleven when I entered the ward. I found George sitting up, seated in a large easy chair, that had been given me by an American missionary, on his visit to the island, who had received it from a governor in India. When poor George took sick, I sent it up to the hospital for his use.

"He was surrounded by a number of his Christian fellow soldiers, and two or three civilians; Sergeants Wright, Noble, M'Calley, and, as I think, Cooper, were there, and brother James Buchanan—all brought to God through the opening of the mission on that island. As I approached, George held out his hand, caught mine with eager grasp, held it for some time, and, gazing upon me, said, 'Mr. Bertram, I 'm glad that you have come; you are my father in the gospel; but for your preaching, I might have lost my soul.' I said, 'George, how do you feel to-night?' His answer was, 'Oh! sir, very poorly;' and, lifting up his eyes to Heaven, he said, 'I thought my Heavenly Father would have sent His chariot of love for me before this time; it has not come yet, but I am waiting for it. I am prepared for it, and all ready to go.' I sat down beside him, and supported his head for some time with my right hand, holding sweet and delightful conversation with him. 'George,' said I, 'Do you feel the Saviour still precious to your soul? Do you still feel that you love Him much?' 'Yes,' said he, 'and I long to be with Him.'

"We then all knelt together at the throne of grace, one of the Christian brethren supporting George in the chair, while I commended his soul, for the last time, to the protecting and everlasting arms of the Redeemer. The earnest spirit of George accompanied us, in his fervent breathings to the throne of grace, and while beseeching the Saviour to be with him in passing through the valley.

"When prayer was over, I sat down at the foot of one of the beds of the hospital, and, being wearied with the exercises of the day, I fell asleep. I slept, perhaps, the greater part of an hour. The conversation, that passed while I slept, was related to me by one of the Christian brethren. He said that it was of the most heavenly and sublime character, which he was altogether inadequate to represent.

"He was not permitted, however, to enter the New Jerusalem, without a vigorous assault from the last enemy. During the first part of the time, his conversation with the brethren bespoke his full assurance of hope, and a soul filled with the joys of the great salvation; but during the latter part of the time, a dark cloud seemed to steal over his soul, and envelop his spirit in darkness, as if the light of the Divine countenance was withdrawn. In dismal distress and horror, he began to sink in deep waters where there was no standing; and in the disquietude of his spirit, to cry out to his Christian brethren, 'Oh! what shall I do? oh! what shall I do?' The brethren replied, 'Why, George, what is the matter with you? What has come over you now? Are you not happy now, George?' 'No,' said he, 'I 'm wretched; I'm miserable; I am undone for ever; I 've lost my Christ; He has gone away from me; oh! what will I do for my Christ? Oh! where shall I find my precious Christ? Oh! dear! dear! I have lost my Christ! He has gone away and left me. Oh! what shall I do for my Christ?' The brethren reminded him of the precious promises of the gospel, and betook themselves to the throne of grace in prayer, that the enemy might not be permitted to exact upon him, nor the son of the wicked one to afflict him.

"Prayer prevailed; the enemy was driven back; the snare of hell was broken; the darkness was scattered; the light of God's countenance burst upon him like the noonday sun through an ocean of storms. His soul was radiant with the divine glory; his very eyes sparkled with heavenly joys; 'the peace, that passeth all understanding,' beamed in his very countenance, and again he cried out aloud, 'I 've found my Christ; I 've got my Christ; I have my Christ;' clasping his arms across his breast, with his eyes raised to heaven, he continued to exclaim, over and over again, 'Oh! my precious Christ! What a sweet, lovely Christ! I will keep my Christ. Oh! I shall never part with my Christ. I 'm safe now—I'm happy now; and I am all right with my Christ.' Turning to the brethren, he said, 'I was miserable when I lost my Christ. Oh! I could not live without my Christ. I should be lost, but for Christ. But now I 'm happy with my Christ.' He said, 'Brethren, are you all happy? I am so happy, I think I could spare some of my happiness. Am I dying, brethren? Is this dying? Why, I feel as if I was in heaven.' While he thus spoke, the cough seized him, and convulsed him for a length of time. It was evident to all that it was death, storming, and shaking, and demolishing the earthen tabernacle; it was his last struggle with the last enemy. When the coughing fit was over, he was only able to say, 'Brethren, lay me down on that couch there, on the floor.' Four of his Christian fellow soldiers removed him from the chair on which he sat, and laid him on the mat. All now gathered around him, kneeling and stooping over him.

"Such a sight my eyes never beheld. Soldiers, with their red coats, and epaulets, bending over this Christian hero, in his last great conflict with the king of terrors! He opened his eyes once more, and his last words were, 'Victory! Sweet Jesus! Precious Jesus!' His head fell over, and the soul of the victorious warrior, shouting from the battle-field, had fled."

"JAMES F. H. BERTRAM, youngest son of James M'Gregor Bertram, a beautiful boy in person, intellectual, talented, and exceedingly affectionate, the hope and delight of his parents, was removed from them suddenly, and at a time least expected. James was brought up, from his childhood, in the 'nurture and admonition of the Lord.' At the domestic altar, unceasing prayer was offered for his salvation. He was instructed in the good way of the Lord; to read His word, to respect His laws, and to keep His holy Sabbaths; nor was he inattentive to divine instruction, but felt, in some measure, his obligations to God; had, however, like all other boys, faults and sins, which, when pointed out to him by his parents, by way of rebuke and correction, grieved him much and afflicted him sore. On those occasions, he would retire to his room alone, confess his sins before and to the Lord with a broken and a penitent heart. It was touching to hear him sobbing and begging God to pardon and forgive him for Jesus' sake, and make him a good boy. Mr. Janisch and his father were in the habit of giving public lectures to the children in the mission house, which were in general well attended and blessed of God. On one occasion, after Mr. Janisch had delivered one of his lectures to the children, James came into the parlor, his heart full to overflowing. Grief seemed to choke his utterance. At length he sobbed out, 'Oh! father, you should have heard Mr. Janisch to-night; what good things he did say.' He was evidently convinced of sin, awakened, and deeply concerned for his soul's salvation.

"He retired into his room, fell on his knees, and earnestly pleaded with God for mercy and for a new heart. He continued at this exercise for two hours together, until it grew late in the night; and in this state of mind he was put to bed. The death of George M'Nought affected him sore. He was well acquainted with George, and loved him much, for he was already a lover of good men; and, when George died, James, in the depth of his sorrowful heart, was one of his chief mourners, and wept for him much. Some time after the death of George, sufficient time for its solemnities to have passed away, James was one evening found, after he had been put to bed, crying bitterly—so much so, indeed, that neither his mother nor any one in the house could comfort him. His mother came to his father, desiring that he would go in and see him, speak with him, ascertain the cause of his grief, and comfort him.

"He went to his bedside, and asked, 'James, what is the matter with you? What aileth thee, my dear boy?' But his dear little heart was too full of grief at once to answer. At last he sobbed out and said, 'Father, I am crying for George M'Nought.' 'Why,' said his father, 'my dear boy, should you cry for George? You know George was a good man, and died happy in the Lord, and is now in heaven.' He said, 'Father, I know that; but I am crying, too, for my own soul.' His father told him, he was glad to hear that he was concerned for the salvation of his soul.

"He then entered into a lengthened religious conversation with him, talked to him of the nature of sin, of the guilt and danger of sinners, of the love of God in the gift of His Son, and of the love of Christ in the gift of Himself, in suffering, bleeding, and dying for us.

"He then pointed out to him the necessity of an atonement for our sins; the nature and the efficacy of that atonement; the necessity of the agency and influence of the Holy Spirit, to apply the blood of Christ, to change and regenerate the heart; and also pointed out to him the way of justification by faith; exhorted him to believe on Christ, for the salvation of his soul—free pardon and acceptance with God, for the witness of the Spirit, and for adoption into the divine family. All this he pointed out to him in the plainest and simplest language possible, and by the most easy and natural illustrations, such as his tender mind might be able to comprehend. To all this he listened with serious and eager attention; and when his father would ask him if he understood all these things, he would answer 'Yes,' or nod his assent. Thus he endeavored to point the soul of his dear child to the Lamb of God, who taketh away the sin of the world. Once or twice his father knelt down and poured out his soul to God in prayer for him; during those supplications, he was earnestly engaged with God for himself. When prayer was ended, he seemed comforted and composed, and shortly afterward fell asleep. What work the blessed Spirit of God wrought in his soul that night, cannot be known; but it was very evident, that a work of grace had begun in his heart, which was to fit and prepare him for a better world. Shortly after this he returned from school during the hot weather, complaining of his head, which continued worse and worse, until he betook himself to bed, from whence he never rose.

"He had every medical aid and strict attention from his good and able physician, Dr. John Stewart, whose kindness to the child during his illness will ever be held in grateful remembrance by the parents.

"Little James' trouble was all in his head. He seemed to be swallowed up with sleep, from which it was difficult to arouse him even for a moment. Hence he spoke little during his illness; but, when asked if he loved the Saviour, with firmness he would answer 'Yes,' and then fall off to sleep again.

"They will never forget the kindness of the little church of God on Ocean Rock, in this their severe trial of faith and sore affliction. By the church, prayer was made to God, without ceasing, for the salvation of both body and soul of James. For him hundreds, if not thousands, of earnest prayers had ascended to the throne. Thus the church continued to cry to God in his behalf until his soul was transplanted from the prayers of the Church militant on earth, to join the songs of the Church triumphant in Heaven. He was the first after the death of George who followed him to heaven, and now sleeps in the dust of death, on the Rock of the Ocean, at the feet of that mother in Israel, Mrs. Sarah B. Judson."

C.

MISSION TO AMERICA

The Church of St. Helena have reason to be grateful, not only for the kind providence which brought Mr. Bertram to their shores, but also for his temporary absence. The object which they had in view has been accomplished, and more. Through the representations of their pastor in his numerous addresses, they have been introduced into the fellowship of the churches in Africa, Europe, and America. Their history was previously altogether unknown beyond the narrow circle of their own sea-girt isle, and, in most cases, their very existence had not come to the knowledge of God's people in other portions of the world. Now they are known, honored, and loved wherever their pastor has gone, and will be remembered with deep interest by many thousands.

A brief relation of the incidents of Mr. Bertram's agency will form a proper sequel to the account already given of his life and labors.

A few days after the public meeting, in which he bade adieu to his devotedly-attached people at James' Town, Mr. Bertram, his wife, and daughter, embarked on board the brig Velox once more, now under the command of Captain Ware, on their way to Cape Town. After a long passage of twenty-nine days, they reached the Cape in the latter part of March, 1850. They met with a hearty welcome from the kind friends of former days, under whose auspices they had undertaken their mission to St. Helena nearly five years before.

After some three or four weeks' sojourn at Cape Town, arrangements were made for a public meeting, which was held the last week in April, at Union Chapel (Rev. Dr. Phillip's), when Mr. Bertram " rehearsed all that God had done with them, and how He had opened the door of faith" unto the benighted natives of St. Helena, and many of the residents of that island. In the account given of this meeting, in the " Cape Town Mail," of Saturday, May 4th, 1850, it is said, that " the Rev. Mr. Freeman took the chair, and the Revds. Dr. Adamson, Mr. Stegman, and Mr. Vogelzegang advocated the claims of the mission on the Christian people of Cape Town, with whom it originated, and the necessity of their aiding Mr. Bertram in the accomplishment of the object for which he has visited Cape Town. Mr. Bertram's report was interesting and encouraging

" The South African Commercial Advertiser," also, of May 8th, 1850, observed that " those of the public, who profess to feel an interest in the diffusion of pure and undefiled religion, have an opportunity of evincing their sincerity, by assisting the Rev. Mr. Bertram, in his praiseworthy labors at St. Helena. Mr. Bertram was favorably known here some years ago as a missionary among the large and somewhat turbulently-disposed body of sailors in Saldanha Bay, where some hundreds of vessels, with their crews, were crowded together in that place, removing the guano. He has since been highly useful at St. Helena, and is now engaged in raising funds for the erection of places of public worship in that island."

During his stay of about six weeks at the Cape, about one hundred and twenty pounds ($600) were contributed to this object by the different denominations at Cape Town.

About the middle of May, he embarked with his family on board of the schooner Avon, Captain Webb, for Boston, in the United States of America, where he arrived, after a passage of fifty-six days, on the 10th of July, simultaneously with the lamented decease of the late President of the United States, Zachary Taylor.

He had been kindly furnished with the following testimonial from the American Consul, William Carrol, Esq., a member of his congregation, but not a communicant, from the first; and from whom, as Mr. Bertram testifies, he had continued to receive, even to the last, the most pleasing proofs of kindness and regard; to whom, also, not a few of the missionaries who have stopped at the island, have been in like manner indebted.

"St. Helena, *Feb.* 18, 1850.

"Rev. Rufus Anderson, *Missionary Rooms, Boston.*

"Rev. and very Dear Sir,—This opportunity serves for me to introduce to you the Rev. James M'Gregor Bertram, who has been carrying out the work of the Lord in this island for the last five years; and happy I am to tell you that in my belief he has done more real good in that time than has been accomplished for the last one hundred and fifty years.

"Mr. Bertram's object in paying your liberal country a visit, is, to get his cords strengthened, about which he will no doubt communicate with you freely; and I pray you to extend to him the right hand of fellowship, and to give him that Christian support and help which, in my conscience, I sincerely believe he deserves.

"To write more on this subject, would be to write volumes, which is unnecessary, as he will give you a faithful account of himself and his operations, and will further explain the various obstructions and hinderances he has had to contend with in preaching the unsearchable riches of Christ in this place. Through your help and influence, I trust he will be enabled to return back soon to his work. I therefore recommend him to your Christian sympathies and kindness, and that of your friends, and remain,

"Rev. and very dear sir,
"Yours, most respectfully,
"W. CARROL."

Similar testimonials had been furnished him from H. E. Rutherford, Esq., a distinguished Christian merchant of Cape Town, and one of the truest friends of missions, and of all such enterprises, to be found in the Southern hemisphere; long known to the American missionaries in that portion of the world, as the Financial Agent of the American Board.

"CAPE TOWN, *May 15th*, 1850.

"REV. DR. R. ANDERSON,

"DEAR SIR,—I take the liberty of sending you a few lines at the request of my friend, Mr. James M'Gregor Bertram, who has been very useful as a preacher of the gospel at St. Helena. We have done what we could to assist him here; but he requires further aid to carry out his intentions, and will, I trust, meet with such aid in your noble country.

"Our respected friend, Dr. Phillip, is in tolerable health of body, but grows very feeble. His mental powers, with the exception of memory, are still vigorous.

"I am, Rev. and dear sir,
"Very respectfully yours,
"H. E. RUTHERFORD."

He soon found himself among the friends of the Redeemer, by whom he was sincerely welcomed to America. He had the pleasure, also, of finding, at Boston, his friend the

Rev. Jonathan Wade, with whom he had formed so delightful an acquaintance and fellowship at St. Helena, and who now gladly embraced the opportunity of making some return to Mr. Bertram for the many kindnesses shown to him and his lady on their way from Burmah in 1848. In the testimonial and recommendation with which Mr. Wade introduced him to the American churches, he gave an account of what he himself had seen in St. Helena, of the fruit of Mr. Bertram's labors, and said, "May the Lord give him that favor with the pastors and churches in this land, which he and his people have shown to many a poor, worn-out missionary, Baptist and Pædo-baptist, who have stopped, strangers, and otherwise friendless, upon the island."

He was furnished, also, with a general letter of recommendation by the pastors of the Baptist churches in Boston and vicinity, in which they cordially commended his object, and spake in the highest terms of his labors of love at St. Helena. Similar letters were kindly given him by the Rev. Rufus Anderson, D.D., and the Rev. S. L. Pomeroy, D.D., Secretaries of the American Board of Commissioners for Foreign Missions; and by the Board of the American Baptist Missionary Union.

Thus furnished, he entered upon his agency; and in the course of the next ten or eleven months, visited the churches of different denominations in and about the city of Boston, the principal cities and towns of Massachusetts, New Hampshire, Rhode Island, and Connecticut, being everywhere received with a cordial welcome by Congregationalists as well as Baptists, and exciting everywhere a deep interest in behalf of the "Lone Isle" of the South Atlantic. He was favored, also, with liberal contributions to the cause, not more from the Baptist denomination than others. The question was hardly asked, "To what sect do you and your church belong?" It was Christ's work in which he was engaged, and as such he was recognized and received by the friends of Christ.

It would be invidious to particularize the names of distinguished pastors, in the various places that he visited, from whom he received the most flattering and encouraging letters of commendation. It will be sufficient to refer to the letter of his excellency, George N. Briggs, the Chief Magistrate, at that time, of the Commonwealth of Massachusetts, whose kind and Christian attention to the missionary stranger will never be forgotten. Governor Briggs wrote as follows:

"I have had the pleasure of an introduction to the bearer, the Rev. James M'Gregor Bertram, a missionary at St. Helena. He is now in this country to solicit pecuniary aid for the establishments which, under Providence, he has been instrumental in building up on that island. The testimonials of his character are entirely satisfactory. His position, the success of his labors heretofore, his kindness and attention to missionaries from this country, of different denominations, on their way to and from their stations, give him strong claims upon the liberality of American Christians.

"Most cordially I commend him to the friends of faithful missionaries, and the lovers of the great cause in which they are engaged.

"Geo. N. Briggs.

"Pittsfield, Mass., *24th Dec.*, 1850."

As the summer of 1851 approached, Mr. Bertram found it necessary to intermit, on account of his health, which had suffered somewhat, the arduous and wearying labors of his agency. He also desired greatly to revisit his native land, and the scenes of his youthful days. Accordingly he took passage on one of the Cunard steamers at New York, in the month of June, 1851, for Liverpool, whence, after a pleasant and speedy voyage, he went up to Dumfries, to see his kindred according to the flesh, and was of course received as a welcome visitor. His companion had preceded him some weeks previously. They also visited Newcastle-upon-Tyne, and Manchester, in both of which they had formerly resided. At Manchester they had the pleasure of receiving a note from the High Sheriff of St. Helena, S. Solomon, Esq., a man of high standing and great respectability. In this note the sheriff says, "All goes on well at the mission house. Indeed, you laid the foundation, and, no doubt, all will prosper. Your exertions to promote the welfare, demands public thanks. God grant you health and long life to follow up your undertaking."

Five or six weeks having been passed very pleasantly in Great Britain, they left their native shores once more, on board the New York packet ship "Jacob Westervelt," Captain Hoodless, August 20th, 1851, for New York city. Ten days out, and not long after they had passed Cape Clear, they were overtaken by a terrific gale, which continued to pour its fury upon the ship and its eight hundred inmates for two days and a night. In this awful storm, the ship was so disabled, by the loss of her main and mizen masts, and rigging, as to be compelled, after the tempest subsided, to put back for repairs to the Cove of Cork, where they shortly after arrived in safety.

The delay of a fortnight in that harbor, gave Mr. Bertram an opportunity of forming an acquaintance, not only with the "Green Isle," but with many of her worthy sons, and of addressing congregations of different denominations in the city of Cork, on the St. Helena Mission. On one occasion, while delivering an address in the meeting-house of the Rev. Benjamin Young, a Baptist minister of Cork, the house, and windows particularly, received the questionable benefit of a shower of stones, but without any corporeal damage to the ministers or people.

Embarked again on their westward way, they reached the port of New York in safety, under the guidance of their Great Protector, and with hearts of devout gratitude, on the 12th day of November, 1851. Here, too, they received a cordial welcome, and Mr. Bertram was admitted to the pulpits of nearly all the Presbyterian and Congregational, as well as the Baptist churches in New York, Brooklyn, and vicinity. Generous contributions of money were received, and the amount of donations to the object, which previously had reached the sum of $3000, was swelled to nearly $6000.

By the good providence of God, Mr. Bertram hopes to return, in the course of the summer or autumn, to his lone island home, bearing with him, or having sent before him, the full amount of funds which he sought to secure for the erection of the chapels at Sandy Bay and Rose Bower, and to redeem the chapel at James' Town from the mortgage with which it has for years been incumbered. But this is by no means the whole of the burden with which he will be freighted. He bears with him the sympathies, prayers, and lively hopes of the thousands of God's people, whom, by God's favor, he has interested in his work, of which this humble volume is a feeble testimonial.

THE END

Late Publications.

Nights and Mornings,

Or Words of Comfort addressed to those who are sowing in tears and shall reap in joy. By JOHN DOWLING, D. D. "Weeping may endure for a night, but joy cometh in the morning." CONTENTS:—1. Nights of weeping and mornings of joy. 2. Night of conviction and mornings of conversion. 3. Night of desertion and morning of restoration. 4. Night of trouble and morning of deliverance. 5. Night of weariness and morning of Rest. 6. Night of death and morning of everlasting life.

Sketches of a Tract Missionary.

BY REV. GEO. HATT.

This is a volume of experience, of facts and incidents in the path of personal effort.

The wrong side of the Line,

OR JUVENILE INFLUENCE.

BY J. H. ROSS.

A good book for Boys and Girls.

The Marriage Memento;

A treatise on the nature of Matrimony, the mutual obligations of husband and wife, with appropriate instruction to both,

BY REV. S. REMINGTON.

Some are put up with a neat marriage certificate, folded in like a a map, for the use of ministers to present those they marry. Price from 12½ to 75 cents, according to the style of binding.

Memoir of Afred Bennet, Senior,

AGENT OF THE AMERICAN BAPTIST MISSIONARY UNION.

By REV. H. HARVEY. 12mo. Price, 75 Cents.

THE

LIFE OF ALEXANDER CARSON, LL.D.

BY REV. GEORGE C. MOORE.

OPINIONS OF THE PRESS.

(From the Independent, N. Y.)

Mr. Moore has rendered a good service to the memory of his preceptor by this sketch of his private and inward life, and he has rendered also a service hardly less valuable to Christian truth and charity.

(From the Religious Herald, Richmond, Va.)

This is an interesting work. Indeed, it could scarcely fail to be so, for its subject was not only one of the most learned and able theologians of our own denomination, but one of the great men of the present age.

(From the New York Tribune.)

The biography of that eminent scholar and divine in a style of unusual vivacity and point.

GIFT-BOOKS,

IN PLAIN AND ELEGANT BINDINGS,

FOR SALE BY

EDWARD H. FLETCHER,

141 NASSAU STREET, NEW YORK.

MISCELLANIES.

BY WILLIAM R. WILLIAMS, D.D.

Plain 12mo, $1 25; do. 8vo, $1 75; half morocco, $2 25; cloth, full gilt, $3 00; Turkey, full gilt, $5 00; do., clasps, $6 00.

DOWLING'S CONFERENCE HYMNS.

Plain, 25c.; gilt, 40c.

THE LIGHT OF THE WEEK:

Or, tne Advantages of the Sabbath to the Working Classes.

A PRIZE ESSAY.

Plain, 25c.; cloth, full gilt, 60c.

PROVIDENCE UNFOLDED.

BY ALEXANDER CARSON, LL.D.

Plain, 75c.; cloth, full gilt, $2 00.

LIFE OF ALEXANDER CARSON, LL.D.

BY REV. GEO. C. MOORE.

Plain, 60c.; cloth, full gilt, $1 50.

WORDS IN EARNEST.

AN EXCELLENT WORK FOR THE YOUNG.

Plain, 75c.; full gilt, $2 00.

MEMOIR OF JACOB THOMAS, MISSIONARY TO ASSAM.

Tur. morocco, $2 00.

THE CONVERSATIONAL COMMENTARY

COMBINING

THE QUESTION-BOOK AND EXPOSITION.

DESIGNED FOR THE USE OF SABBATH-SCHOOLS AND FAMILIES.

Vol. I., on Matthew.
Vol. II., on John.
Vol. III., on the Acts.

BY WILLIAM HAGUE.

"The plan of Dr. Hague in these several books to meet the wants of the higher classes in Sabbath-schools, we have never seen surpassed nor even equalled by any other author, according to our taste and judgment."—*Christian Chronicle.*

"It is a species of Commentary quite original, combining all the most valuable results of archeological and critical learning, without the lumber and parade which often render the perusal of the ordinary Commentaries and 'notes' an onerous and unwelcome task. Mr. Hague's plan renders everything clear, impressive, and practical, so that the mind is held, by an increasing interest, to those truths which are most important to be remembered."—*Western Watchman.*

"The method of imparting instruction in this book is a novel but happy one. The author remarks in his preface, 'The teacher who would give instruction in any department of knowledge so as to awaken in his scholar a spirit of inquiry, cannot easily satisfy himself with abrupt and insulated questions; in order to arouse the mind to action and bring himself into sympathy with it, he must *communicate* something. The remark which imparts knowledge, quickens thought, and then conversation proceeds with a rational and easy flow.'"—*Michigan Christian Herald.*

RECOMMENDATIONS

OF

THE KNOWLEDGE OF JESUS.

BY DR. CARSON.

[From the Primitive Church Magazine, London.]

"IN illustrating this glorious theme the author's mind expands in the full strength and vigor of its conceptions, and pictures realities of Divine truth almost too brightly to be beheld with the eye of faith undimmed.

"The present volume ('The Knowledge of Jesus') is full of invaluable principles, cast in an attractive mould. Every page lives with interest; there is no thing dry, nothing tedious. Its style flows transparent and free as the mountain stream."

[From the Orthodox Presbyterian, Belfast.]
EDITED BY DR. EDGAR.

"On matters of church order, it is well known we differ from him; but as a scholar we honor him—as a Christian brother we embrace him. In the knowledge of the philosophy of the language, he is far in advance of the present age; and with respect to metaphysical acuteness and powers of reasoning, he has been called 'the Jonathan Edwards of the nineteenth century.' His character as a philosophic theologian, and a profound, original, independent thinker, stands in the very highest rank; and he is only justly designated, when called one of the most philosophic reasoners of the present age."

www.ingramcontent.com/pod-product-compliance
Lightning Source LLC
LaVergne TN
LVHW050516100826
845148LV00002B/355

9781425521387